FOUNDATIONS OF CLASSICAL BALLET

PERFORMING ARTS

Dance Section
Editor-in-chief: Professor Flavia Pappacena

AGRIPPINA VAGANOVA

FOUNDATIONS OF CLASSICAL BALLET

Translated from the Russian by Aleksandr Wilansky
Edited by Bruce Michelson

GREMESE

Acknowledgements

Alessandra Alberti *dedicates her work to Mauro Martini.*
Flavia Pappacena *wishes to thank Carla Pappacena, for her invaluable col-laboration, and Alessandra Alberti, for her support and friendship, without which it would not have been possible to realize this work.*

Original title: Основы классического танца,
Iskusstvo, Leningrad-Moscow, 3rd edition, 1948.

On the cover: Agrippina Vaganova in 1937,
with A. Shelest, M. Samseva, M. Grishkevich, N. Fedorova.

Original illustrations: Pavel Gontcharov.

Translation from the Russian: Aleksandr Wilansky
Translation from the Italian: Bruce Michelson

Photo design:
Graphic Art 6 s.r.l. – Rome

Printed in USA
by Edwards Brothers

Copyright of the English-language edition:
2014 © GREMESE
New Books s.r.l. – Rome

ISBN 978-88-7301-767-7

TABLE OF CONTENTS

INTRODUCTION TO THE
ENGLISH-LANGUAGE EDITION
by Flavia Pappacena

The centerpiece of our work here is the complete and unabridged translation of the third edition of Agrippina Vaganova's celebrated book, which was originally released in 1948, three years before the author's death. In this edition, which has remained virtually unknown in Europe and America, Vaganova carried out various modifications and also integrated substantial new sections of correlative text, while leaving intact the general design, the illustrations by Pavel Gontcharov and the opening premise from the first edition of 1934. Her additions were, specifically: a new introduction, new references to choreographic production and didactic activity, and a second sample lesson, accompanied by the musical models prepared by S. S. Brodskaya. The results were a broader, more insightful text than its predecessors and a greater balance between technical analysis, choreographic contextualization, classifications and personal memories, including all that was later filtered out during transcription into English. We refer here not only to the first edition by Kamin Dance Publishers, published in New York in 1946, which had already been unburdened by the removal of Vaganova's original preface, with its incisive references to Enrico Cecchetti, Pierina Legnani and her own teachers, but also to the successive English-language edition (A. & C. Black, 1948), released by Dover of New York in 1969 – the version generally referred to until now by students and followers of the Vaganova Method.

In the Dover edition, which relied on a translation by Anatole Chujoy, further alterations were made to the text, reducing the manual to a collection of technical explanations and theoretical-stylistic reflections, with few links to the context from which these were born and reduced reference to the prolific Russian-Soviet theatrical and cultural *milieu* of the period, of which Akim Volinsky and Lyubov Blok were active supporters. Many significant passages of the main text were either relegated to the notes, or, in some cases, dispensed with entirely, which left Vaganova's reasoning incomplete. In addition, even though the second sample lesson from Vaganova's third edition was included, the criteria applied to the graphic arrangement were those of the fourth Russian edition (posthumous), which abandoned the original page alignment – reinstated here in the present edition – that had rendered the material so useful to both dance professionals and ballet accompanists alike. And, while the book may have seemed to gain wider relevance through the adoption of generic words like "student", or "pupil" – already in evidence in the first American edition – this obscured the fact that the book's primary "destination" was originally intended to be a girls' course.

This third Russian edition was the product of the experience Vaganova had gained during a fundamental decade of her pedagogical activity, beginning in 1934 when she began to work at the Technicum (formerly the Imperial School), instructing for the teachers' training course. In this context, Vaganova left her indelible mark, which was not, however, limited to the strict confines of the Leningrad School itself, but rather, reached out to all of Russian dance, including that which was practiced and taught – as she herself remarks – in the most distant regions of the nation. Already near the end of her life, Vaganova put her hands to a fourth edition, but she would not have time to see it go to print. In that edition, she had planned to introduce only small changes, leaving the third version of 1948 practically unaltered. A copy of the third edition, with Vaganova's handwritten notes for a fourth edition, was deposited at the Theater Museum in St. Petersburg.

All this has convinced us of the need to restore to the dance world, after two previous editions in English, Vaganova's final reworking of her manual. In it, the author, already in her late sixties, brings across to the reader how she communicated and expressed herself in the studio, creating the same full range of emotional impact through her juxtapositioning of dry explanatory language and sometimes severe remonstrance with a more personal tone and a wide range of vividly figurative images such as the "crawling plants" on p. 119, the "soft energy" of pas de chat on p. 145 and the "peculiar charm and coloration" of pas failli on p. 156. And she shares the reflections that led to her terminological innovations, including her devotion to the reforms introduced by Vladimir Stepanov, which inspired her revisionary classifications of the positions of the arms and legs.

ABOUT THIS TRANSLATION
by Bruce Michelson and Aleksandr Wilansky

The Russian language is varied and subtle. Words, expressions and ideas that read utterly clearly in Russian cannot always be translated on a one-to-one basis into English. Particularly in these difficult cases, we have sought to capture as nearly as possible the intent, spirit and voice of the author, while maintaining clarity and usage that is commonly understood by dancers and educators in the English-speaking world. There are numerous inconsistencies in the Russian text, and Vaganova changes tone often, switching, for example, from dry explanatory language or stern admonition to a more colorful or personal tone, sometimes within the same section, and she also jumps frequently between direct and indirect instructions. Through it all, she seeks and probes language as a means to communicate sometimes complex movement ideas, and this is complemented by her warm complicity and sometimes unexpectedly playful humor, and the evident deep love she felt for her "girls". Whereas this was largely obscured in earlier translations, here, we have attempted instead to capture as many of these variations and personal touches as was feasible to do, rather than create a more homogenous text where none exists.

In our efforts to achieve accuracy and remain true to the Russian text, while rendering it more readily comprehensible to the English-language reader, we have employed several "instruments". For example, while rounded parentheses are reserved for those used by Vaganova, we have deployed square brackets in order to: clarify the text or its intention; complete its meaning (for example, with verbs that are clearly implied in the Russian text, but unexpressed); or point out the literal translation, where this may either read awkwardly in English if used alone in the main text, or would likely be misunderstood – or, in some cases, not be understood at all.

Vaganova is usually very specific in her descriptions; however, she does at times use certain words in a generic, and therefore, approximate sense, and this is usually in line with common usage at the time in the Russian dance world. Examples of this include the use of "circle" (instead of semi-circle) for *ronds de jambe par terre* or the word "ligaments" when sometimes referring generally to the connective tissues of the foot, and the use of the word "tension" to indicate the work of the upper part of the arm. Further, it should be noted that the Russian word for "leg" is the same as that used for "foot", and therefore, certain passages have necessarily been adapted to reflect a correct interpretation of the actions described – in particular, where the "leg" is bent, and the "foot" (not the leg) touches the other knee, for example. The outmoded use of the term "half-toe" has been updated to the more current "demi-pointe", and similarly, references to "pointed toes" have generally been rendered as "pointed feet". Where errors appear in the original text, these have generally not been corrected in the main text – for example, in the description of glissade (p. 156), where her explanation of the change of weight "from the right leg to the left" appears inconsistent with the previous text.

Terms written by the author in French, as well as the many French terms that are transliterated into Russian, have been rendered in French, as is common in the language of ballet, with the exception of the word "pas", for which the English equivalent "step" has often been used, where applicable. Phrases that are written partially in Cyrillic and are not specifically French – "большой adagio" (bolshoi adagio), for example – have generally been translated into English; in this case, "big" adagio instead of "grand" adagio.

In her introduction (p. 35), Vaganova points out that, after careful consideration, she opted for simple language as used in the classroom over technical terminology, and we have applied this same principle to other instances, as well. In the explanations of musicality in the sample lessons, for example, we have chosen standard, easily comprehensible English usage (beats, half-beats and quarter-beats), in place of Vaganova's standard Russian usage (quarters, eighths and sixteenths). This principle has also been applied more generally to certain phrases that, in Russian, reflect normal usage, but read awkwardly when translated literally into English; in these cases, we have most often opted for normal English usage over strained literal translation, although in certain passages, we felt the need to sacrifice this principle, as the images summoned up by the Russian text are specific, indispensible and/or simply irresistible.

For the transliteration of Russian names, we did not feel it proper to adopt the newest methods for a historical book such as this, and we have therefore remained faithful to mid-20th-century models, which often give a more precise indication for English readers as to the Russian pronunciation.

In her introduction to 1st position of the arms, Vaganova writes that "they should be supported from the shoulder to the elbow by work [lit.: tension] in the muscles of the upper arm." It is important to see phrases such as this in their proper context, and we note that Vaganova was not advocating here a stiffening of the arm muscles, but rather a lifted and supported position, in contrast to what she considered the drooping arms of the French School of the period.

As regards the original index, while we would have wished to preserve both its form and its substance, numerous adjustments were necessary in order to make it relevant and useful for today's reader.

We wish to thank all those who have supported our efforts, in particular Claudia Bisagno, the late Ian Richardson, and Donald Francis, for his invaluable musical expertise.

AGRIPPINA VAGANOVA, DANCER AND TEACHER

by Flavia Pappacena

In her comprehensive profile of this great Russian artist, Russian critic Lyubov Blok[1] bears witness as to how, already in the 1930s, Agrippina Vaganova's style had come to be widely identified with that of her students, and how the memory of the "incomparable" performances by Vaganova the ballerina had, by then, already been lost.

Vaganova's "perfection", Blok explains, had been formed over time, through a gradual stratification of knowledge and experience, upon which Vaganova proceeded to carry out her own intelligent and detailed personal research[2]. She had been admitted to the Imperial School in 1889, at the age of ten, and she studied there with Aleksandr Oblakov, Lev Ivanov, Ekaterina Vazem and Christian Johansson, all exponents of the French line which was dominant in St. Petersburg at the time. She then graduated under the guidance of Pavel Gerdt during the same year in which the class of Enrico Cecchetti was established, and despite the great desire of the Italian *maestro* to have her among his students, she was not admitted, as she was already in her last year of studies.

Like her whole generation, however, Vaganova was strongly affected by the presence of the Italians in St. Petersburg[3], in particular by the teachings of Cecchetti and the technical-virtuoso model formulated by Pierina Legnani from La Scala, who had burst onto the scene at the Maryinsky at this time. Upon entering

---

[1] Lyubov Dmitriyevna Blok, *Klassichesky tanetz. Istoria ee sovremenosst*, Iskusstvo, Moscow, 1987. Blok (1818-1939) is cited in the text, as are Akim Volinsky (1861-1926) and Vladimir Stepanov (1866-1896). Both Volinsky and Blok were fervent admirers of Vaganova.

[2] See: Preface [to the first Russian edition].

[3] See: Appendix by Alessandra Alberti.

the company, Vaganova studied with Olga Preobrajenska, a student of Cecchetti, acquiring a series of notions and techniques which she then consolidated and expanded under Nicolai Legat[4], who, having been Legnani's partner[5], taught Vaganova many of the Italian ballerina's secrets. Then came her artistic encounter with Fokine and her memorable interpretation, in 1910, of the Mazurka in *Chopiniana*.

The quality she attained in the later years of her career – when she succeeded in obtaining the coveted titles of Soloist (1905) and then Prima Ballerina (1915) – was marked by a technical and formal accuracy that remained undiminished when confronted with difficult challenges, and it stemmed from a highly informed approach to the rules – those same rules, the most profound significance of which, as Blok writes, Vaganova wished to penetrate. Her specialty, remembers Blok again, was the jump: a high, light jump – like that of a bird, Petipa had commented – easily detached from the floor and suspended in the air with that *ballon* of which she writes with such emphasis in the relative chapter. This quality, supported by tenacious study, allowed her to perform and master such difficult steps as the cabriole front, in which she attained maximum elevation – as high as that of a male dancer – and grand jeté, which she executed without the usual auxiliary movements, jumping directly from the preceding step. Her beats were so quick, clean and well-crossed that her entrechat-six barely left the floor – an uncommon characteristic at the time – giving the impression of unusual lightness and brilliance. The reknowned critic Akim Volinsky, remarking on the superiority of her jump – even higher than Pavlova's – remembers how, after having launched herself into the air without the aid of introductory movements, Vaganova would manage to remain suspended "for some seconds", with her body still and upright.

---

[4] Legat, a Soloist at the Maryinsky from 1888, later became First Dancer. He also worked there as Assistant Balletmaster, starting in 1902, and then, from 1905 as Second Balletmaster, and as First Balletmaster from 1910. He was also Principal Teacher at the Imperial School in St. Petersburg from 1888 to 1914.

[5] Blok considered both Vaganova and Shavrov as students of Nicolai Legat.

As Vaganova also remembers, Volinsky, at whose school she also taught during the first years of her didactic activities at the Theater, would have a determining influence on her stylistic maturation. Traces of this influence are to be found in many passages of the book, and not only where the critic is respectfully quoted. The frequent contact with Volinsky, Legat and Fokine, as well as the influences that emanated from Isadora Duncan's presence in Russia, all served to sharpen the ballerina's awareness and accelerate the stylistic and technical transformation that turned Vaganova into one of the exemplary figures in Russian classical ballet during the early 20th century – a protective custodian of classical tradition, yet also a modern, educated woman, sensitive to the demands of a new era and conscious of the need for a renewal in dance education. This aspect emerges in numerous passages, particularly in the preface, where she underlines the importance of a cultural education for dancers, with the implication that this includes studies in theater history, art history, music history and also dance history.

From the very beginning, Vaganova's work was aimed toward a creative synthesis of the French and Italian Schools, in order to resolve and surpass the (already by then) anachronistic dichotomy that existed between the two styles. Without renouncing the technical proficiency of the Italian dancers, and still preserving the color and refinement of the traditional Russian School, she distilled the teachings of the old masters – those formed along the lines of the French-Danish School – stripping away their affectations and didactically inconclusive practices and conceiving instead a new and extremely rational pedagogical line, which was verified through the anatomical-scientific knowledge introduced by Vladimir Stepanov and constructed upon a didactic program that, although inspired by that of the Italians, was free of the inflexible schematics of Cecchetti and La Scala, which was regarded at the time as more of a factory than a school. She preserved and indeed improved upon both the clarity and the plasticity of the lines elaborated early in the 19th century by Pierre Gardel and Carlo Blasis, fusing these together with the picturesque tastes of Saint-Léon and Petipa, and harmonizing them with the aesthetics of new Soviet culture.

The results were quickly noted by both public and critics. Valeria Chistyakova, who later authored the introduction to the posthumous fourth Russian edition, recalls press comments filled with admiration and even stupor upon the first appearance, in 1925, of the seventeen-year-old debutante Marina Semyonova: virtuosity, a rich orchestration of movement, speedy turns, unusually expressive and melodious arms, and an agile body.

All these qualities are to be gathered from Vaganova's book. The *arabesques*, reduced to four and condensed into a concise, modern vision, are structured on a strong counterweight between torso and legs, as in Romantic ballet; but here, they also display a dynamic curve of the back that should be as evident to the spectator as the expressive thrust of the body and arms. The *épaulements*, which place the body in strongly angular positions, appear to be a fusion of the strong-willed *attitudes* from character dancing and that heroic attitude of the new protagonists of the Soviet stage. The *en-dehors* and *en-dedans* of the torso, with its soft, deep bends, present anew – from a modern aesthetic viewpoint – the principles of "abandon" and "counterweight" that had been transmitted by Blasis in the early 19th century in order to bestow a grace upon the movements, stabilize the weight and experiment with new forms of balance.

All these elements demonstrate how Vaganova placed the idea of *the body*, as it had been understood in classical tradition, at the center of dance expression: the body as a harmonious totality, constructed upon an informed balance between rationality, emotion and physicality.

Genealogical Tree:
Teachers of the St. Petersburg School
by Lyubov Blok

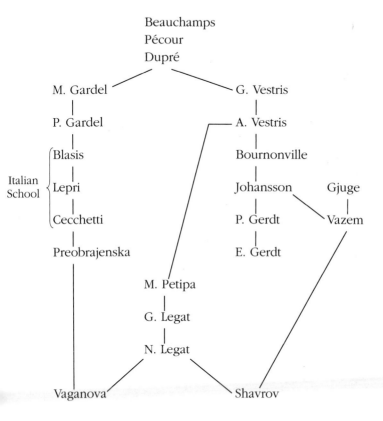

CHRONOLOGICAL SUMMARY
OF THE LIFE OF AGRIPPINA VAGANOVA
by Alessandra Alberti

1879 – Born Agrippina Yakovlevna Vaganova in St. Petersburg on June 26. Her father, Yakov Vaganov, is an usher at the Maryinsky Theater.

1889 – Admitted to the Imperial Ballet School, where she studies with Aleksandr Oblakov, Lev Ivanov, Ekaterina Vazem, Christian Johansson and Pavel Gerdt.

1890 – Stage debut in the premiere of *The Sleeping Beauty*, choreographed by Marius Petipa, as one of the Cupids who pull the Lilac Fairy's coach.

1897 – Graduates from the Imperial School.
Enters the corps de ballet of the Maryinsky Theater, where she debuts in the ballet *Mlada*, with choreography by Marius Petipa.
Begins to study with Olga Preobrajenska.

1904 – Birth of her son Aleksandr.
Petipa leaves his post as First Balletmaster of the Maryinsky Theater.

1905 – Promoted to Soloist of the Maryinsky Theater Ballet.

1915 – Promoted to Prima Ballerina.

1916 – Leaves the Maryinsky Theater Ballet due to age limits, but continues to dance as a guest artist in other theaters.

1917 – Begins to work as ballet teacher, first at the school of Baron Miklos, and later at the school of Akim Volinsky.[1]

1921 – Begins to teach the lower and intermediate level courses at the Petrograd State Theater School (formerly Imperial Ballet School).

---

[1] Valeria Chistyakova, in her introduction to the fourth Russian edition, which was included in the 1969 publication by Dover, maintains that Vaganova began to teach at Volinsky's school in 1918, while Vera Krasovskaya and Stanley Rabinowitz both confirm that Volinsky opened his school in 1920.

1922 – Invited to teach the "classe de perfection" at the State Academic Theater of Opera and Ballet (GATOB), known from 1935 as the Kirov Ballet.

1931 – Appointed Artistic Director of the Ballet Company of the State Academic Theater of Opera and Ballet, a post which she will hold through 1937.

1934 – On her initiative, the pedagogical department at the Technicum (formerly the Petrograd State Theater School and from 1937, the Leningrad Choreographic School – the school that now bears her name) is opened, and she is appointed Head of this new department, a post she will hold until 1941.

Receives the title "People's Artist of the Russian Soviet Federal Socialist Republic".

Publishes *Osnovy klassicheskogo tantsa* (Foundations of Classical Ballet).

1938 – Having left her post as Artistic Director of the Kirov Ballet, she continues to teach at both the Kirov Theater and the Leningrad Choreographic School.

1943 – Receives the title Professor of Choreography. Becomes ballet consultant to the Bolshoi Theater in Moscow.

1946 – Teaches at the Pedagogy Department in the Leningrad State Conservatory (through 1951).

Receives the Stalin Prize of the First Class.

1951 – Dies in Leningrad on November 5.

1957 – The Leningrad Academic School of Choreography is named after her. (Since 1991, it has been known as the Vaganova Academy of Ballet.)

MAIN ROLES (in chronological order)

(in parentheses: choreographer / composer)

Corps de Ballet Roles

Mlada (Petipa / Minkus, Rimsky-Korsakov; *The Daughter of the Mikado* (Ivanov / Vrangel); *Giselle* (Coralli, Perrot / Adam); *La Bayadère* (Petipa / Minkus); *Don Quixote* (Petipa, Gorsky / Minkus, Drigo); *The Sleeping Beauty* (Petipa / Tchaikovsky); *The Little Humpbacked Horse* (Saint-Léon, Petipa, Ivanov,

Gorsky / Pugni); *Les Caprices du Papillon* (Petipa / Krotkov); *Swan Lake* (Petipa, Ivanov / Tchaikovsky); *Raymonda* (Petipa / Glazunov); *Nutcracker* (Petipa, Ivanov / Tchaikovsky); *Harlequinade* (Petipa / Drigo).

SOLOIST ROLES

Black Pearl in *The Pearl* (Petipa / Drigo); Oread the Nymph in *Cupid's Pranks* (Ivanov / Friedman); Cygnette in *Swan Lake*; two Fairy variations in *The Sleeping Beauty*; Imene in *Acis and Galatea* (Ivanov, Kadlets / ?); Gypsy and soloist in Grand Pas Classique in *Paquita* (Petipa / Minkus); Gypsy in *Esmeralda* (Perrot, Petipa / Pugni, Drigo); Grand Pas d'Action in *Cinderella* (Petipa, Ivanov, Cecchetti / Fitinhof-Schell); Three Odalisques in *Le Corsaire* (Mazilier, Perrot, Petipa / Adam, Pugni, Delibes); Hebé in *Flora's Awakening* (Petipa, Ivanov / Drigo; the River variations Yellow, Rhine and Thames in *The Pharaoh's Daughter* (Petipa / Pugni); divertissement pas de deux in *La Fille mal Gardée* (Dauberval, Petipa, Ivanov / Hérold, Hertel); variation of the Frescoes and Queen of the Nereids in *The Little Humpbacked Horse*; Shade variation (cabrioles) in *La Bayadère*; Chinese Dance in *The Fairy Doll* (N. and S. Legat / Bayer); 2nd Act variation in *Le Talisman* (N. Legat / Drigo); *The Whisper of the Flowers* [solo created for Vaganova] (N. Legat / von Blon); Queen of the Dryads in *Don Quixote*; Pas de Trois in *Paquita*; variation in *Coppélia* (Saint-Léon, Petipa, Cecchetti, Ivanov / Delibes); Waltz and Mazurka in *Chopiniana* (Fokine / Chopin); Butterfly in *Carnaval* (Fokine / Schumann); Clémence and Henriette in *Raymonda* ; Frost in *The Seasons* (Petipa, N. Legat / Glazunov); Orchid in *The Scarlet Flower* (N. Legat / ?).

Principal Roles

Naila in *La Source* (Saint-Léon / Minkus, Delibes); Odette-Odile in *Swan Lake*; The Tsar-Maiden in *The Little Humpbacked Horse*; Giselle in *Giselle*.

CHOREOGRAPHIC CREATIONS

Swan Lake (1933); the original Ivanov version of Act II was retained.

Esmeralda (1935); the pas de deux of Diana and Actaeon appeared in Act II.

MAIN STUDENTS

Marina Semyonova, Galina Ulanova, Tatiana Vecheslova, Olga Mungalova, Nina Mlodzinskaya, Elena Tangieva-Birzniek, Vera Kaminskaya, Olga Iordan, Natalia Dudinskaya, Feya Balabina, Nina Anisimova, Vera Stankevich, Antonina Vasilieva, Elena Chikvaidze, Valentina Lupokhina, N. Zheleznova, Zinaida Vasilieva, Galina Kirillova, Nadezhda Krasnosheyeva, Alla Shelest, Svetlana Sheina, Nonia Yastrebova, Lyubov Voisins, Maria Mazun, Ludmila Safronova, Ninel Kurgapkina, Olga Moiseyeva, Irina Gensler, Ninel Petrova, Alla Osipenko, Irina Kolpakova. She also taught Maya Plisetskaya for few months in Moscow.

PRINCIPAL PUBLICATIONS OF THE BOOK

1934 – First edition
1939 – Second Russian edition
1945 – *Las Bases de la danza clásica*, Centurión, Buenos Aires
1946 – First English-language translation: *Fundamentals of the Classic Dance (Russian Ballet Technique)*, Kamin Dance Publishers, New York (reprinted 1948, 1956)
1948 – Third Russian edition
1948 – *Basic Principles of Classical Ballet*, A. & C. Black, London
1951 – Publication of Czech and Hungarian versions
1954 – *Die Grundlagen des klassischen Tanzes*, Henschel, Berlin (reprinted 1981, 1987, 1994)
1962 – Fourth Russian edition (posthumous)
1969 – *Basic Principles of Classical Ballet*, Dover Publications, New York (reprod. of the edition by A. & C. Black)
1976 – *Basi principali del balletto classico. Tecnica russa del balletto di Agrippina Vaganova*, Tersicore, Milan
1981 – *Il metodo Vaganova*, Di Giacomo, Rome
1993 – *Principes du ballet classique*, Editions IPMC, Paris
2007 – *Le basi della danza classica*, Gremese Editore, Rome
2014 – *Foundations of Classical Ballet*, Gremese Editore, Rome
2014 – *Les bases de la danse classique*, Gremese Editore, Rome

SELECTED BIBLIOGRAPHY

Balet Entsiklopediya, Sovietskaya Entsiklopedia, Moscow, 1981.

Degen, Arsen and Stupnikov, Igor, *Leningradsky Balet 1917-1987, Slovarh-sprabotshnik*, Sovietsky Kompositor, Leningrad, 1988.

Krasovskaya, Vera, *Vaganova, A Dance Journey from Petersburg to Leningrad*, University Press of Florida, 2005.

Pawlick, Catherine E., *Vaganova Today. The Preservation of Pedagogical Tradition*, University Press of Florida, 2011.

Rene (Roslavyeva), Natalia, "*Khniga Vaganovoy zha rubezhom*", in Volkov, N.D. and Slonimsky, Yuri, *Agrippina Vaganova. Stat'i, vospominanya, materialy*, Iskusstva, Leningrad-Moscow, 1958, pp. 295-308.

Volinsky, Akim, *Ballet's Magic Kingdom* (edited by S. J. Rabinowitz), Yale University Press, New Haven and London, 2008.

Vaganova in the pas de trois
from *Paquita* (1912)

Vaganova in the solo variation
from *Le Talisman* (1909)

Vaganova in the waltz/mazurka from *Chopiniana* (ca. 1910-14)

Vaganova in the role of Odette in *Swan Lake* (1913)

Vaganova during class, with Ninel Kurgapkina and Ludmila Safronova, ca. 1945-46

Plaque inscribed with the name of Agrippina Vaganova at the entrance to the Choreographic School in St. Petersburg

А.Я.ВАГАНОВА

ОСНОВЫ КЛАССИЧЕСКОГО ТАНЦА

ИЗДАНИЕ ТРЕТЬЕ, ИСПРАВЛЕННОЕ И ДОПОЛНЕННОЕ

Главным Управлением
учебных заведений
Комитета по делам искусств
при Совете Министров Союза ССР
рекомендуется как учебник для
хореографических училищ

ГОСУДАРСТВЕННОЕ ИЗДАТЕЛЬСТВО

«ИСКУССТВО»

Ленинград—Москва
1948

PREFACE
[to the first Russian edition]

The task at hand in our theater is the tireless research into new forms of ballet performance, which is a response, on the one hand, to our new [Soviet] cultural content, and on the other, to the need for the preservation, through critical analysis, of our received classical heritage.

We carefully defend our classics, yet time rolls on, and all things can be improved. Inevitably, we dancers ever strive to reach perfection. Every day, we face the same material in our exercises, and, as a result, we constantly and progressively refine our technique. The drive to advance is inevitable; we are drawn forward by the pace of life itself.

However, our preserved classical heritage is not determined solely through technique. The perfection of form – this is the main beauty of the old ballets, and it is this that we must preserve and develop. To understand this perfection, to discover the [special] features of classical ballet – now that is a fascinating challenge. Working over the method of teaching, I have endeavored to set down the basis for a science of dance, as well as the achievements [derived] from my many years of experience as a dancer and teacher.

Naturally, my knowledge did not arise out of nothing; it was formed and shaped. When I look back, I see, first of all, the beginning of my early work in the theater, the first year after school. Back then, in the '90s, there were still some antiquated dance traditions that had been established at the end of the previous century. When the Italian dancer Cecchetti appeared on the scene, two systems were successfully in use: the French and the Italian. Leading the Italian School were Cecchetti and a whole series of virtuoso touring soloists, among them, [Pierina] Legnani, who had settled permanently in our theater. The teachers in our school and all the company basically adhered to traditional French schooling, which, by that time, was showing signs of decline: slackness in the poses, unfeeling arms with sagging elbows, weak execution of the virtuoso steps. Neither I, nor my colleagues [lit.: anybody] heard inspiring words from our teachers that would awaken our creativity. "Legs, legs! Be more flirty!" – this was the sort of remark our longtime teachers would make. At the same time, Cecchetti – who was a typical exponent of the Italian style – had a teaching method in which the poses were all vigorous and dynamic; the arms were either extended strongly or sharply bent, properties that gave a clear expressiveness to the dance. This stylistic difference caught my attention and made me think.

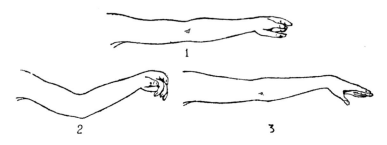

Fig. 1. *1* – Russian; *2* – French; *3* – Italian

After leaving school, I struggled for a long time with my arms – which were positively awful. "Arms, arms!" I heard shouted at me from all sides; but nobody showed me or explained to me what I should actually do with my poor "arms"! Then I had an opportunity to work a bit with an exponent of the Italian School. During training, she held her arms taut and extended. In response to a remark from one of my comrades, "What is this stick?" she calmly replied that, "This way, [the arms] will not hang and dangle helplessly, with nothing to say." This conversation started me thinking about the differences between the dance schools, and focused and sharpened my powers of observation; and, over time, my creative pursuits have led me forever away from the indifferent dance of "Legs, legs!" At first, I adopted her way of holding the arms, but of course, I could not be content with just this; there were still no methodological guidelines on the work of the arms in her style. I carried out the complete re-education of my arms alone and in my own way, and I developed on myself the method for mastering the technique of the arms that I now use in practice.

Comparing, observing and searching for new possibilities of further development, I entered the second phase of my stage career already equipped with a developed technique, which I found necessary to call "my" technique, because, despite the many influences, it neither repeats, nor copies from any other school. It is a continuation and development of the Russian classical ballet tradition.

Some of my contemporaries and younger colleagues have gone through a similar evolution, and since the first decades of the 20th century, one no longer finds either the French or the Italian School in its pure state here on our stages.

My teaching career began in 1917 and has evolved together with the growth of Soviet society and culture. These conditions have favored any original development of creative forces. My pedagogical knowledge has come to be widely used, and I have been able to create an entire generation of young artists who are responsible for the finest work in all our theaters.

This book is an account of my experience, my achievements and my teaching method. It is a textbook of classical ballet and, at the same time, a practical guide for young dancers and teachers who, being far from the major centers and with no access to personal assistance, wish to reinforce and refresh their knowledge.

For these two reasons, I have chosen to use the simplest everyday language – familiar in the classroom and familiar to the ear – without complicating it with scientific and pedantic terms or figures of speech.

In this way, also the non-professional reader will find it more easily understandable and more accessible, should he or she wish to become acquainted with some details of classical ballet. Interest in classical ballet continues to grow year-by-year among a wide range of public, and I think that such an accessible exposition of its theory and practice is timely.

In view of the massive cultural development in our country and the need to educate new ballet teachers, the Education Department of the Leningrad Order of Lenin Conservatory, where I work, was founded, in order to train young teachers, based mainly on the classical ballet method I have developed.

In the gathering of literary materials, as well as the design of the first edition of this book, extremely valuable assistance has been rendered to me by L. D. [Lyubov Dmitriyevna] Blok.

FROM THE AUTHOR
[introduction to the third Russian edition]

In this third edition of my book "Foundations of Classical Ballet", some additions and corrections have been made, as well as an additional sample lesson, this one with musical accompaniment.

The use of French terminology for classical ballet – as I have emphasized in all discussions on this subject – is inevitable, for it is international. For us, it is the same as Latin in medicine: it has to be used. When the Italian Cecchetti was working in England during the last years of his life, he [also] used this same terminology, which was as much a foreign language to him as to his students, but absolutely international and universally accepted. However, I must now bring in one caveat: that not all of our terms coincide with those accepted by the French. For several decades, our dance has developed without any direct contact with the French School. Many names have disappeared, some have been altered, and finally, our school has introduced new ones. But they are all variants of a common, international system of dance terminology.

As regards my describing of the forms of classical ballet, I have chosen an order that will be convenient for those who wish to acquaint themselves with classical ballet as a whole. Therefore, I have combined the descriptions into groups of general concepts – battements, jumps, turns, and so on. This order is completely unrelated to the order in which they are learned, but gives a simple systemization of all the material. In each chapter, the descriptions of the steps proceed from the simplest form to the most advanced and difficult, so as not to complicate their use in teaching according to the class program.

Those who wish to become acquainted with the sequence in the lesson, with the combination of steps as accepted by myself and my colleagues, will find this information in the chapter on lesson construction and in the accompanying examples.

When describing a step, I speak of the *right* foot as being front, or of the right leg beginning a movement, only so as to not interrupt the text each time to say that *the movement can also begin with the left leg*. I do this for the sake of brevity and to avoid overloading each description with superfluous phrases. It is done for the sake of convenience and has no other significance.

I have also tried not to repeat the description of any method of execution already described in an earlier explanation of another step. The reader who comes across an unfamiliar expression should refer to the index and read its description on the specified page.

In most cases, I have given a description of the step in its full form, *in the centre* and with arms; if the accompanying illustrations show a step at the barre, the arm movements may easily be added from the description in the text.

To indicate the directions [lit.: degrees of turn of the body], I have adapted the system used by Stepanov in his text *Alphabet des Mouvements du Corps Humain*, giving it however a more general interpretation.

It seemed to me more sensible to change to a more convenient numbering, using the following order:

1) center [down-]stage, 2) front right corner, from the dancer's viewpoint, 3) center of the wall to the right, and so on (fig. 2b).

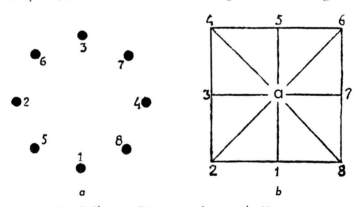

Fig. 2. Classroom Diagram: *a* – Stepanov, *b* – Vaganova;
a – center; the student may refer to this page for all of the examples described in this book.

Anatomical method is used to measure the angle formed in the lifting of the arms and legs – that is, in relationship to the body's vertical axis – also taken from Stepanov's book. We use this notation for the legs, and when we say, in general, that a leg is raised to 45°, 90° or 135°, we speak of the angle formed between the leg and body, depending on the individual dancer. In other words, a "90°" angle does not always correspond to a mathematical 90°; it is a symbol used to indicate a horizontal position of the leg, with the toes at hip-level.

I hesitated at length as to whether to take the exact terminology from anatomy and biomechanics* – so succinct and convenient to use – to describe the various parts of the body, legs and arms, and for the designation of directions and body planes. In the end, however, I rejected the idea, knowing that these terms are rarely used in the dance world. But I will use some specific words in the anatomical sense, such as thigh, shin, shoulder, forearm, frontal plane, etc., and I hope that the reader will understand me, instead of giving these words their everyday or some arbitrary meaning. So, although obviously a bit rough in terms of phrasing, I prefer to write each time: "the upper leg from the hip to the knee; the lower leg from the knee to the toe", etc. The description may be cumbersome, but this eliminates the possibility of any misunderstandings.

It should be added that, in order to achieve full coordination of all the movements of the body in the dance exercises, it is necessary to inspire the movement with both thought and feeling [lit.: mood] – i.e., to give to them that value which we call *artistry*.

I do not touch this theme in this manual but work on it daily with great care in lessons for the advanced classes and in the Classe de Perfection.

Translator's note: The reference here is to the movement method for theater developed by Vsevolod Meyerhold (1874-1940), which had great currency at the time and remains in use in Russia today.

LESSON CONSTRUCTION

I often have to point out that we approach the study of any step gradually, from its most basic form to its ultimate expression in dance.

The same gradual approach is taken in the mastering of the whole science of dance – from the first steps to dancing on stage.

The best lessons do not unfold in their entirety all at once: they begin with exercises at the barre, then [continue] *in the centre* with adagio and allegro.

When children begin their studies, they do the exercises at the barre and *in the centre* only in their driest form, without any variation. Subsequent exercises introduce simple combinations at the barre, which are then repeated *in the centre*. These replace the simplest barre exercises. Next comes a light adagio, without difficult combinations, aimed only at acquiring stability.

We then make the poses more complex by introducing the work of the arms, and in this way, we gradually come to complex adagio combinations.

All of the movements that I describe from here on in their simplest forms are executed later on demi-pointe.

Finally, after the adagio combinations, we introduce jumps, which bring the students to their ultimate perfection [fulfillment of their training].

In the adagio, one masters the placement of the body and head. Begun with the simplest movements, adagio becomes infinitely more complex and varied over time. In the final class years, difficult, complex combinations are introduced one after another. To do these, the students must have been thoroughly prepared by the previous classes, mastering their bodies and their stability, so that when faced with new and greater challenges, they do not lose their control. Such sophisticated adagios develop agility and mobility of the figure, so that when one faces the big jumps in the allegro, time will not have to be wasted on mastering the body.

I want to pause at allegro and highlight its very special significance. In it, one sees the science of dance, all its complexity and the promise of future excellence. All of dance is built upon the allegro.

To me, the adagio does not reveal enough. The dancer is helped here by the support of her partner, by the drama or lyricism of the stage situation, and so forth. Today, a lot of virtuosic movements can be inserted into the adagio; however, they all depend in large measure on the partner's skill. But to go out and make an impression in a variation – this is another matter: here is where we see the impact of a dancer's education. Not only the variations, but most of the solo and group dances are built upon the allegro; all the waltzes, all the codas – they are all allegro.

All of the work that precedes allegro is only a preparation to dancing, but when we come to the allegro, it is then that we [truly] begin to learn how to dance, and this is where all the wisdom of classical ballet is revealed to us.

Children dance and jump in a burst of fun, but their dancing and jumping are simply instinctive manifestations of joy. To turn this into art, style and artistry, we must give it some form; and this process begins with the study of allegro.

When a student's legs are correctly placed and well turned-out, when the sole of the foot has been developed and strengthened and has gained elasticity, and the muscles have been strengthened – then one can begin to study allegro. The study of jumps begins with temps levé, in which one returns to the floor on two feet in 1st, 2nd and 5th positions, then comes changement de pied, and finally, échappé – all helped at first by facing the barre and holding it with both hands.

The next jump, which, as a rule, is quite complex in its structure, is assemblé – and there are deep and compelling reasons for this tradition.

Assemblé forces one to immediately work all the muscles properly. It is not easy for the novice to learn; you need to carefully control every moment of the movement, eliminating even the possibility of any sloppiness or muscular laxity in doing this *pas*. The student who has learned how to do assemblé correctly has not only learned the *pas* itself, but has also acquired the foundation for the performance of the other allegro steps – these will seem easier, and there will be no temptation to do them loosely. If correct alignment and body control are assimilated from the earliest steps, they will become habit.

It would be infinitely easier to first teach a child to do, for example, balancé; but how can we instill in the child the right way of holding the body and controlling the muscles? Because this step is so easy, the student's legs weaken and relax unintentionally, and they do not acquire turn-out, as is learned in assemblé. The difficulties inherent in assemblé lead directly to the goal.

After assemblé, you can go on to glissade, jeté, pas de basque and balancé, which, I repeat, it is advisable not to introduce until the muscles have been well-developed in the basic jumps, and the jump has been given its proper foundation.

Then, knowing how to do jeté, it is not at all scary to go on to [other] jumps onto one leg (those in which, after the jump, one foot is either sur le cou-de-pied or open), for example, sissonne ouverte in the various directions.

Along the way, you can teach pas de bourrée, although it is done without leaving the floor, but needs firmly placed feet.

At this stage, one can begin to give the student some easy dances.

In the senior classes, the students study the most difficult jumps, with a suspension in the air, such as saut de basque, for example. Of these, the most difficult one – cabriole – completes the study of allegro.

I repeat, I discuss allegro in general and dwell on it, because it is the foundation upon which all of dance is based.

In the more senior classes, when the lesson needs to become increasingly complex, all the steps can be done en tournant, or turning. Ranging from simple battements tendus to all the complex adagio and allegro *pas*, everything is done en tournant, to give yet more difficult work to the already strengthened and developed muscles.

As regards the construction of lessons, I will not give any fixed schemes or firm rules; this is an area where the decisive role is played by the experience and sensibility of the teacher.

In our times, in this period of rapid development, life

abounds in the theater, and the pace has nothing in common with the old times. Previously, each student and artist performed maybe three or four times a month. Now, the number of performances has increased significantly. You've got to be very careful.

If a given class or group of dancers are noticeably overworked, [or] if I know that they are overburdened by their work, sometimes I will give them only light work in class for a couple of weeks, leading the students with greater care. However, if – what a relief! – they have less work to do, or some event has lifted the energy, and they feel the possibility of more strenuous effort, then the lessons become energized, and I use this time to load them with more difficult exercises. In short, we must be very sensitive to the working conditions, so that the lesson itself does no damage. If I dictate any program, I would like it not only to be executed, but also exceeded. But nonetheless, my duty is to teach my students to work well without sacrificing their health.

The same principle is valid for students who are given work in a production. Just like any student working in a factory, our students refine their knowledge through direct practice in the theater. Here as well, we should not set any fixed rules. Depending on the needs of the productions, the students are sometimes asked to do on stage what they have not yet learned in the class curriculum and is not in the class program. You cannot impose any restrictions or dry rules here either. The theater presents its requirements to the school, and these can be satisfied, without doing harm to the students, when the teachers demonstrate a sensitivity and knowledge of their students: if it [what the theater asks] is difficult for one student in the class, there will be others who can do it. In this regard, the balletmaster should confer with the teacher and correct the students according to the teacher's instructions. If we were to have the students follow the teaching program slavishly while they are gaining practical stage experience, it could inhibit their artistic development and the growth of individual talent.

Because of all this, I believe it impossible to place any rigid schemes on the lessons – this business demands absolute individualization and consideration of the various circumstances.

However, I will say this about the work of artists and their daily lessons and preparations for performance: that we should approach the daily training as we approach a [medical] treatment – we get a prescription, but in general, everyone knows how he should apply it in order to treat himself.

Occupational injuries to the legs are extremely common among dancers; and in order to find the best way to return the affected area back to working condition, their training must be ordered differently; it is not enough to just "warm up" before you can safely return to the level of work necessary for performance.

Here, I consider it useful to mention that I quite agree with the existing conviction among many dancers of the benefits of training during the summer heat. I heartily recommend to my girls not to stop doing their daily exercises in the summer. For one can make great strides during those short summer months, and I have seen this many times. No time is wasted in "warming up" the legs, as they are already "warmed up" before the lesson, are more receptive and gain more benefits from any efforts – you can proceed directly to the more difficult work, which is very beneficial for the development of the ligaments and flexibility of the joints.

I will limit myself to a few general guidelines for conducting the lesson, and at the end of the book, the reader will find examples of my lessons, tailored to students of the senior classes.

From the first year of study until the end of a dancer's working life on stage, the daily exercise is composed of the same steps. Of course, by the end of first year, the student does not yet do all of the exercises, but even the smallest child, just beginning to learn, is already doing those movements which will later become part of the dancer's full exercise program.

The following is the order of the steps (except for first year students, who do them in a different order).

Exercise begins with pliés in the five positions.

Here, I will digress a bit. The fact that one starts with pliés in the order of positions – that is, beginning with 1st position – is neither an accident, nor just a silly tradition. Although there are those opinions maintaining that it is better to start with pliés in

2nd position, I cannot go along with them. It may seem easier to learn to do pliés initially in 2nd position, as it is more stable, but this approach has its drawbacks; due to the steadier balance in this position, when studying this plié, control of the body is easily forgotten, and proper concentration on the wholeness of the body lost. Therefore, it is better to begin the study of plié in 1st position, where the less secure footing requires one to make quite some effort from the beginning, in order to maintain that vertical axis around which all balance and dancing is built, and where we are forced to hold our muscles – to not let the buttocks stick out when bending the knees and to keep the whole figure more compact. This correct position provides the foundation for every plié. It is all much more difficult to achieve in 2nd position, even for more advanced students, and the risk is even greater with beginners; children can easily become accustomed to working with loose muscles, whereas what we are trying to achieve is control and stretched legs from the very first demi-plié.

After pliés come the battements tendus. From the earliest classes, the battement tendu must develop such a sound and strong turn-out that later, in jumping, the legs assume a distinct, correct 5th position by themselves; because, by this point, there will no longer be any chance to correct this. To do this, it is necessary that, from the very first steps, the foot is placed neatly and tightly into 5th position every time; only then can a correct 5th position enter into the dancer's flesh and blood.

After the battements tendus come: rond de jambe par terre, battement fondu, battement frappé, rond de jambe en l'air, petit battement, développé and grand battement jeté.

Almost any step can be combined and made more complex, according to the class, the teacher's approach and the method used in the school.

I will say just that, in the elementary grades, it is not necessary to fill the time with too many varied combinations for the children. Exercises can be tedious in their uniformity, though one can break the monotony by doing movements in different tempi (½ time, ¼ time), changing them around so that the children are not doing anything mechanically, but instead following the music. In these classes, the foundations of muscle development and elasticity of the ligaments are being introduced, based on these initial movements. All this is achieved through the systematic repetition of one movement a considerable number of times in a row. For example, it is better to do one step eight times in a row than to do two to four combinations in eight measures. A few scattered movements will not achieve our goal. We must be absolutely sure that the student has mastered the movement and will do it correctly in all the combinations, and only then can one add complexity to the lesson without doing harm. Otherwise, we will perhaps only expose the cleverness of the student, but the legs will remain weak, and none of the steps will be assimilated to the end.

In brief, if you force a lot of poses on the children at the expense of the technical development of movements, their development will proceed slowly. In the intermediate grades (V and VI), it is permissible to use combinations, but also with great care, for we must not forget that these classes are for the dancers to build the greater strength needed to allow them to concentrate all of their attention in the senior classes on the development of the dancer's art.

Dancing abilities should be developed by working equally on the movement of the arms and legs. If [however] the focus of attention is on the legs and arms alone – and the body and head are forgotten – one will never achieve total harmony in movement or create a proper impression in performance. What happens then is that the execution is calculated toward a cheap effect, and if one poses the arms excessively and forgets about the legs, then again, full movement harmony will not be achieved.

In the senior classes, the exercises at the barre may seem relatively shorter in time, but this is deceptive. All of the exercises in the senior classes are the same ones that are done in the lower grades. But owing to the more advanced technique, they are taken at a faster pace and therefore take less time, while still managing to give the desired elasticity to the muscles.

Exercises *in the centre* are combined from the same steps as for the barre, and then we move on to the adagio and allegro.

Here, I must make one general remark.

In recent years, there have been some radical changes in the allocation of teaching time in our school, due to new guidelines that require of future Soviet artists a broader outlook and greater versatility in the study of their respective specializations. In our school, we offer them the opportunity to test their strengths not only in the classroom, but also in practical experience – participation in ballets and the performances at the school. The students do not feel cut off from their future artistic life; from their earliest experiences, they find out what they can and should take away from the lesson, and so, they learn how to study conscientiously and seriously. This opportunity for total development, which is now available in our school, plays no small role. There is no comparison between our overall program today and the old programs, both in the general curriculum, as well as in the specialized fields.

In my time, the study of character dance was nearly inexistent; it was learned along the way from dance numbers. Exercises for character dance were developed during the 1920s by A.V. Shiryaev, who systemized the movements of character dance and greatly facilitated the work in this area.

Not to mention subjects such as history of theater, art history, history of ballet, music history, etc.: in my time, these subjects were not in the program, as it was not considered necessary for a dancer to have a theoretical background for her ballet career.

To all of the above, it should be added that live demonstration is necessary to achieve perfection in the choreographic art. "Our kind of" art form is difficult to convey accurately in a textbook.

Time and again, I have thought of Pushkin's verses:

"One foot touching the floor, the other slowly circling –"

In our language, it is as if one foot does rond de jambe en l'air, while standing on the toes of the other (i.e., with the leg firmly supported on the tips of the toes). Or perhaps she is not doing rond de jambe en l'air, but playing with her leg in a grand rond de jambe at 90°; because of what it says, "slowly circling". And further:

"And then a leap, and suddenly she flies –"

Fly where? Upward, or rushing away? This is so beautifully written, but unfortunately, it is difficult to translate these poems by Pushkin into movement – they reside in the realm of fantasy.

In order to preserve all of our achievements for posterity, we have found it necessary to resort to the services of a cinematographer, and this will be a great contribution to the perpetuation of our art. As the years pass, we hope that our achievements, captured on film, will bring great benefits and that these films will help future generations to learn and improve.

Our first experience in this will be shown in the near future to the general public – it will consist of images of classical dance technique at the Moscow and Leningrad Choreographic Schools. This film will benefit academic growth and aid schools in the outlying regions.

THE FORMS OF
CLASSICAL BALLET

I. CORE CONCEPTS

POSITIONS DES PIEDS

The five basic positions of the feet are well-known. Five, because no matter how hard you wish, you will not find a sixth position with the legs turned-out from which it would be convenient and easy to move. There are turned-in positions ("les fausses positions"), with the toes facing inward, and there are half turned-out positions of the feet, used in the study of historical dance. But "les bonnes positions" (turned-out) are the core of classical dance.

For readers unfamiliar with dance, I offer here a description of the positions of the feet: 1st – both feet are completely rotated outward (turned-out), touching only at the heels, and they form a single straight line; 2nd – the feet are on one line, but there is a space between the heels equal to the length of one foot; 3rd – the feet (turned-out) adjoin at the heels, which come together with the midpoint of the [other] foot; 4th – similar to 5th position, but one foot is opened in the same position [i.e., alignment] forward or back, and between the feet, there is a space of one small step; 5th – the feet (turned-out) touch along their entire length, so that the toe of the one foot touches the heel of the other foot (fig. 3).

Fig. 3. Positions of the feet

BENDING DOWN. PLIÉ

Plié is the common French name for a movement of the legs which, in Russian, is designated by the word "prisedanie" [bending down].

Plié is done in the five positions. At first, it is done to half-depth – the demi-plié – and then on to a full deep knee-bend, or grand-plié, but not before the demi-plié has been mastered.

Plié is inherent in all dance movements; it is encountered in every dance step, and one needs to pay particular attention to its execution in absolutely every exercise.

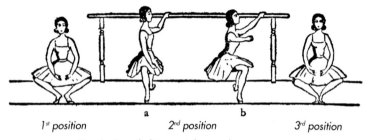

1st position   a   2nd position   b   3rd position

Fig. 4. Grand plié: a – right way; b – wrong way

If one's dancing has no plié, its execution is dry, stiff and devoid of plasticity. However, if this insufficiency in pliés is noticed in a student, these shortcomings can, to a certain extent, be corrected. This is possible through the development of the student's plié by emphasizing this part of every exercise. One who is richly gifted by nature with dancing abilities will have a very supple Achilles tendon, and the [lower] leg easily forms an acute angle with the foot. With others, it [the ankle] hardly bends. If that is the case, it will be necessary to enter into a struggle against the [student's] natural build, and much care and time is needed here. Therefore, if, at the beginning of studies, plié is causing difficulties for a student, and the feet, especially the ligaments, start to become damaged, it is better to postpone the work on plié for a while and return to it after some time, carefully and gradually.

In the study of plié, one should observe the rules that follow, [while] distributing the weight of the body evenly, not only on both legs, but also on the soles of both feet, i. e., without rolling on the inner [lit.: forward] part of foot, something that we often observe with students who have natural knock-knees [lit.: X-shaped legs] (genuvalgum). As with all the exercises, we study pliés at the barre, holding it with one hand (fig. 4).

1) First, we need to carefully study the demi-plié, which is executed without lifting the heels from the floor. We must pay close attention to this, as this keeping of the heel on the floor perfectly develops the tendons and ligaments of the ankle joint. You should not begin to study grand plié directly after demi-plié; but instead, extend the development of the demi-plié through exercises of battements tendus in 1st and 5th positions with demi-plié.

2) In both demi-plié and the deep [grand] plié, it is extremely important to open the knees firmly, i. e., to achieve a full turning-out of the entire leg, and especially to pay attention to the upper part of the leg, from the hip to the knee. The knee always bends in the direction of the toes.

3) In grand plié, keep the heels from lifting off the floor as long as possible. When it is impossible to stretch the tendons of the feet any further, the heels must not detach from the floor with a jerk, but lift away softly and gradually. The heels do not remain off the floor for long; once you begin to rise, lower the heels without any delay.

4) In 2nd position, the heels do not rise from the floor at all, since you can go deep in this position without lifting them. The feet are separated the distance of one foot-length, and this small opening of the legs is most beneficial for the development of their flexibility. In this plié, one should by no means stick the buttocks out, as this gives a wrong form to the movement and does not produce sufficient turn-out in the hip, which should be accomplished by this plié.

5) Having reached the deepest point of the plié, one should not remain there for even an instant, but start immediately to come back up. By remaining "sitting" in the plié, not only do you not develop the pushing strength in the muscles and elasticity of the entire leg, but on the contrary, this weakens these levers of the jump. Dancers call this "sitting in the plié" [lit.: in

the legs]. Just as dangerous to some dancers is to do too many pliés, which can also cause this "sitting" in the plié.

6) The descent to the deepest point in pliés takes the same amount of time as the rise, and it occurs gradually (fig. 5).

Fig. 5. Grand plié in 1ˢᵗ position

When plié is done *in the centre*, the following arm movements are added: before starting the plié, open the arms to 2ⁿᵈ position, passing – as a general rule – through preparatory position and 1ˢᵗ position. When beginning the plié, the hands lift slightly and lower again, with the palms turned downwards.

As the plié reaches its deepest point, the hands meet at a low level. Upon rising, the arms pass through 1ˢᵗ into 2ⁿᵈ position in the same time as the straightening of the legs, with neither haste, nor delay.

These are the arm movements for all the positions (except 4ᵗʰ) when done en face, where we already see the idea of épaulement for croisé and effacé; then 4ᵗʰ position is introduced, and the arms take the following form: if the right foot is front, the left arm is in 1ˢᵗ position and the right in 2ⁿᵈ. When the body is turned (i. e., croisé or effacé), the arms stay in the specified position for the entire plié. With the other foot [front], the other arm is [forward] opposite to the front leg (fig. 6). Subsequently, once control of the arms is mastered, one may do plié with a port de bras.

Croisé   Effacé

Fig. 6. Demi-plié in 4ᵗʰ position and full plié in 5ᵗʰ position

HEAD AND SHOULDERS. ÉPAULEMENT

Épaulement is the first feature of future artistry to be introduced into exercises for beginners and children. Students begin with movements of the legs, done en face[1] until they become accustomed to holding the body steady while doing an exercise, which happens by the end of the first year of training. Then it is already possible to add some play to the body, to introduce a hint of future artistic coloring into [an otherwise] dry exercise.

The usual direction for 1ˢᵗ and 2ⁿᵈ positions is en face. But 3ʳᵈ and 5ᵗʰ positions are already done with a turning of the shoulder: if the right foot is forward, the right shoulder is turned forward, and the head turns to the right. The 4th position allows for a

---

[1] When we speak of the position en face, it means that the body remains facing straight front, in contrast to épaulement (when the body is turned).

dual turning: if you take it in croisé, the right shoulder is forward, and the head is to the right; in effacé, the right foot will be forward, but the left shoulder is forward, and the head turns to the left (fig. 6). Thus, the basic line of classical dance, which is entirely constructed on croisé and effacé, is introduced from the start. The richness of form in dance is derived from these, and this could never blossom so magnificently if we had only the dullish and monotonous position en face.

Speaking of épaulement, i. e., the turning of the shoulders to one side or the other, we must not forget that the direction of the head plays a dominant role in the poses croisées, effacées, écartées, etc., and is an integral element. The ability to turn the neck freely – from childhood on – should be included in the central tenets for any type of dance, not only the classical.

One can sometimes observe in performance that an artist, during the execution of any given *pas*, holds his neck and, with it, the head, in a tense manner; the execution becomes strained, its ease is lost, and there is no clear expression within the general design of the dance. In such a case, the facial muscles are also not participating; they are stuck in one position, neither reflecting emotion adequately, nor doing anything to aid the dancing image.

THE CONCEPTS OF CROISÉ AND EFFACÉ

We have already discussed these two basic positions of classical ballet when speaking of épaulement, pointing out how necessary they are for the development of variety and completeness of form in dance. Here, I will dissect the basic types of poses, croisée and effacée.

The Croisée Pose

Croisé signifies crossing, and the crossing of the legs is indeed its basic attribute. The croisée poses can be either front or back (fig's 7a and 7b).

Croisée front. Stand on the left leg, with the right leg open to the front and the foot pointed, the body turned to point *8* (fig. 2b) and the head to the right – [the gaze] crossing over the leg.

(The left arm is raised in 3rd position, and the right is taken out to 2nd position). This is the basic position croisée front, although the arms and head can also be combined in other ways.

Suppose that you have lifted your right arm up, and the left has been taken to 2nd position – to give this some finish, you can incline your head forward, looking under the right hand.

Keeping the arms as in the above example, you can [also] turn the head to the left, looking under the left hand, or lift the gaze to the left hand, in which case, the head should deviate slightly to the back. With this change of gaze, the facial expression will also change involuntarily: if in the previous poses, the lowered head draws the facial features together, when the gaze is transferred upward, the cast of the facial lines opens up; the expression becomes more relaxed, spiritual. It is highly desirable to introduce these changes of facial expression into the dance as early as possible, in order to avoid an expression that is later forever petrified in an eternally frozen smile, something which we encounter quite often on the stage.

| *a* | *b* | *c* | *d* |
| Croisée back | Croisée front | Effacée front | Effacée back |

Fig. 7

Croisée back. Stand on the right leg, with the body and head facing the same direction [as above] and the left foot pointed to the back. In the basic croisée front pose, the arm raised is the one opposite to the extended leg; here, it is the same arm as the outstretched leg that rises, i.e., the left arm is up, the right is to the side, and the head is turned to the right.

Here, too, one can make various combinations of the head and arms. For example, the right arm can be up, with the left to the side, the body inclined forward, and the head inclined to look under the right arm. You can also raise one arm up and have the other arm closed in 1st position, and so on.

The Effacée Pose

In this pose, in contrast to the croisée pose, the leg is open, and the whole figure is exposed (fig's 7c and 7d).

Effacée front. Stand on the left leg, with the right leg open to the front, the foot pointed, the body turned to point *2* (fig. 2b), the head to the left, the left arm in 3rd position and the right open in 2nd, and the body inclined to the back. This is the basic pose. But the body can also incline forward to look under the left hand, and other combinations are also possible: for example, the hands and arms can be extended outward, etc.

Effacée back. Stand on the right leg, left leg back, with the foot pointed and the toes aimed toward point *6* (fig. 2b). The head, arms and body directions are the same as above, but the body is slightly inclined forward, and the pose assumes an impression of flight. Here, too, further combinations are possible.

TOURS EN DEHORS AND EN DEDANS

En dehors. The concept of en dehors defines the rotary motions going "outward". For everyone involved in dance, this concept – and its opposite, en dedans – is instilled from the very beginning of training. The elementary explanations that I provide here are intended for interested persons who themselves want to understand these concepts, and as a classroom aid for teachers of adult classes, who frequently find it difficult to explain en dehors and en dedans to students who have not studied dance before.

Take the first example of en dehors with which the student is faced from the very first steps: rond de jambe par terre (see description on p. 81). Here, there are no difficulties, as the foot obviously moves to the outside, describing an arc forward, out through 2nd position and to the back.

To understand rond de jambe en l'air en dehors is much more difficult. Beginners are confused by the fact that the foot which has been thrown out to 2nd position at the beginning of the movement moves in a semi-circle apparently inward, drawing the back half of a circle. I have succeeded in explaining quickly and easily the direction of rond de jambe en l'air to my girls who could not understand, as follows. I suggested to them to mentally transfer the rond de jambe en l'air onto the floor. If the foot, in all parts of the circle, goes in the same direction as in rond de jambe par terre en dehors, then we have rond de jambe en l'air en dehors, and vice versa. Then the student will easily understand that, in the en-l'air, she finishes with a movement outward, whereas the par-terre begins [with a movement] outward, but in both cases, the forward arc of the circle is en dehors (fig. 24).

To explain the concept of en dehors in tours and in turns around one's vertical axis in general, the simplest and most elementary explanation will also be the clearest. A turn is en dehors when you turn away from the standing leg, i.e., if I stand on the left leg and spin to the right, this turn will be en dehors; on the other leg, an en dehors turn will go the other way, to the left (fig. 8).

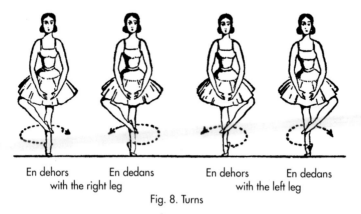

| En dehors | En dedans | En dehors | En dedans |
| with the right leg | | with the left leg | |

Fig. 8. Turns

En dedans. This is the reverse concept – a rotation inward. For rond de jambe, the explanation is similar to that above, with the directions changing accordingly.

In turns, an en dedans turn will be toward the standing leg, i.e., if you are standing on the left leg, you turn to the left; and on the other leg, you do the opposite – turn to the right.

Having learned these basic concepts of en dehors and en dedans in the basic movements, it will be easy to understand the more complex cases, as these will always include an element of rond de jambe or tours.

The concept of en dehors also denotes the turned-out position of the legs used in classical ballet. People who know nothing about ballet say all kinds of wrong and nonsensical things about turn-out; I will therefore clarify, in detail, the origins of turn-out, with the help of some terms from anatomy, although, in general, I avoid using these, in order not to load my descriptions with excessive details.

Turn-out is an anatomical necessity for any theatrical dance – which covers a whole range of movements that are *conceivable* for the legs but *impossible* to do without turn-out. Turn-out requires that the knee is rotated outward much further than is normally possible; and the foot turns out together with it – this being partly a consequence and partly an auxiliary movement, [even if] the whole purpose is to rotate the upper part of the thigh, the femur, outward. The resulting freedom of movement in the femoral joint [hip socket] aids the turn-out, and the leg can be taken more freely to the side; and it also helps in crossing the feet. In normal positions, leg movements are rather limited by the structure of the hip joint. With the abduction of the leg, the femoral neck faces the edge of the acetabulum, making further movement impossible. If you turn the leg en dehors, the greater trochanter retracts, and the lateral flat surface of the femoral neck comes into contact with the rim of the acetabulum, thereby allowing the leg to rise to 90° or even 135°.

Turn-out increases the sphere of action of the leg [in respect] to the volume of the obtuse cone described by the leg in a grand rond de jambe.

This is why strict attention to the en-dehors is central to the training of a classical dancer's legs. It is not an aesthetic concept, but a professional necessity. A dancer with no turn-out is limited in all movements, while a classical dancer with good en-dehors has the full richness of dance movements conceivable for the legs.

STABILITY. APLOMB

To master stability in dance, to develop aplomb, is an issue of primary importance for every dancer. Aplomb is developed throughout the years of school life and is only fully achieved at the end of one's studies. But I believe it necessary to include this as a core concept, as a correctly-placed body is the basis for any step. This must be borne in mind during further studies of the various steps, as their correct execution is founded upon this core.

To develop stability, the dancer begins at the barre: during the exercises, the body should be held straight up on the leg, so that it is possible at any moment to release the hand from the barre without losing balance. This will serve as the introduction to correct execution of an exercise *in the centre*. The standing foot should not roll over toward the big toe, and the body's weight should be distributed evenly across the entire surface of the foot. The body that does not stand directly on the leg, but leans toward the barre, does not develop aplomb (fig. 9). As aplomb improves, exercises progress to demi-pointe and pointe.

When an exercise is done on demi-pointe *in the centre*, stability is aided by the correct positioning of the arms. If the arms do not comply with the positions that I will describe later, it will be very difficult to maintain aplomb. You do not remain stable

c   a   b   d

Fig. 9. Body posture: *a, b* – right; *c, d* – wrong, due to excessive inclination forward and backward

with a sagging upper arm. We describe a dancer as having quite well-developed aplomb when her body is able to maintain a pose standing on one leg for some time.

Such reliable stability is acquired [only] if the dancer can understand and feel the enormous role that the back plays in aplomb. The core of aplomb is the spine. To learn how to feel it and master it, one must carry out close introspection of the sensations in the musculature of the back during the various movements. When you manage to feel and control the muscles of the lumbar region – then you will have grasped the core of all stability. Then the dancer can safely take on the challenges of his/her art, such as the big jumps on one leg (grand jeté and cabriole), for the performance of which the correct way of holding the back is essential.

II. BATTEMENTS

The word battement, in ballet terminology, denotes the outward movement of the leg and its return. In classical ballet, this outward and inward movement has developed into many forms. In considering these forms, we shall become familiar with the essence of this movement.

Fig. 10. Battement tendu simple

BATTEMENTS TENDUS

This battement is the basis of all dance. Its invention was so ingenious that it seems its creator had succeeded in grasping the essence of the structure and function of the various ligaments of the leg. A simple example taken from the dancer's daily life proves how true this is. When a dancer twists her foot slightly while dancing and is not able to put weight on it due to discomfort, she begins carefully to execute a few battements tendus, and the foot is easily restored to full working capability.

It is not without reason that one does battements tendus before dancing, in order to, as we say, "warm up the legs". The legs are not only warmed up through this movement, they are also put in a condition of "perfect fitness" for the upcoming work, especially for the allegro. When you see that a dancer's legs move incorrectly, it is easy to guess that, from the beginning, this dancer has not been raised doing battements tendus exactingly.

Battements Tendus Simples (basic)

For the initial study of this, it is advisable to do this battement from 1st position, as this is less difficult; but we must respect the same rules as for the battement in 5th position, as described below, only, naturally, that the foot has to return to 1st position.

Feet in 5th position, right front. The arms are open in 2nd position[1]. The entire weight [lit.: emphasis] of the body is on the left leg, and the right leg works freely and bears no weight. The right foot slides forward, without taking the toes from the floor. The entire leg is extended as the movement begins, keeping the heel turned outward as much as possible (which gives the sensation of the movement beginning from the heel), and then [the movement] continues with the toes.

If this movement is done carelessly, one often observes that, as the foot slides along the floor and before arriving at the full extension of the toes, it lifts away from the floor, only to rest on it again. Such an execution fails to achieve the proper development of this movement. The legs must strictly maintain the turn-out (en-dehors). In the moment when the foot is returning to the starting position, the heel must be turned-out as much as possible, to arrive in a perfect 5th position. The toes do not follow the movement passively, but emphasize the return to position, toward the heel of the left foot, which gives an artistic finish to the movement (fig. 10).

The same is applied to battement tendu in 2nd position and to the back. When executing this movement in 2nd position, we should see that the right foot continues to draw the straight line of the turned-out left foot. To achieve this, all of the student's attention during the return to 5th position must be directed toward keeping the carefully turned-out heel forward, while the toes strenuously maintain that turn-out. Only with careful turning-out

---

[1] At the barre, the arm is opened to 2nd position before the beginning of the exercise.

of the entire leg, from top to bottom, is it possible to prevent it from moving in a zigzag on the return from 2nd position to 5th position back.

When doing this leg movement to the side, the foot closes alternately in 5th position front and back.

On closing the foot behind, the knee and upper part of the leg must be well pulled up, so that the knee stays fully turned-out and does not bend. It must also be remembered that the leg moves on the same line of the standing leg.

The battement to the back is done with the leg that is behind in the 5th position.

Battements Tendus Jetés

Battements tendus jetés are [essentially] the same as battements tendus simples. Initially, they are studied from 1st position, i.e., the leg is thrown forward and backward in line with the 1st position, and then from 5th position. Having brushed the floor, the leg is thrown into the air at 45° to the front, side or back, with an accent on the closing into 1st or 5th position, while the upper part of the leg (the hip) must not be unduly raised. Without stopping at the outermost point, the foot passes through 1st or 5th position and continues the movement. The French designation for this battement – *jeté* (thrown) – explains the character of the movement.

This battement has great educational value and must be executed with great precision, observing the following rules.

When done to the front, every time the foot passes through 5th position, the toes must accurately touch the heel of the other foot.

The movement to the side should be approached with care, since the main role is played by the turn-out of the working leg; in addition, whether the movement begins from 5th position front or back, the foot must return to the same point in 2nd position each time, the foot being thrown outward to that point precisely, following the rules indicated for battement tendu simple. In the movement to the back, the upper part of the leg once again maintains a careful turn-out. The foot that moves must do so in a way that it is not seen from the front, and the knee must not bend, something that students do inadvertently to make this difficult movement easier. During the return to 5th position, all of the toes absolutely must come into contact with the floor.

I consider it necessary to stress once again the importance of the position of the upper part of the leg. The leg must be "taken away" to the back, and the knee should not fall inward or lose its extreme turn-out. The movement should pass precisely along the floor in line with the standing leg. One must feel one's leg as a taut string.

Battements tendus jetés should be taught once battements tendus simples are executed to perfection and the legs have been strengthened to the point that they are capable of being used freely and without strain.

Battements Tendus pour Batteries (for beats)

These battements are a preparatory movement for beats, particularly for the men, inasmuch as the structure of the male body allows for a slightly different execution of beats, with the upper part of the leg. Women feel the beat more from the calf, although they should try to do it like the men do. But the structure of a woman's build is different, in the shape of the hips and also in the legs, and this prompts a different way of doing beats.

If I use these battements in class, they take the following form:

From 5th position, the right leg opens to 2nd position at 45°, then the right calf beats against the left leg in front, keeping the leg taut and in the same direction, strongly turned-out, then it opens slightly and changes to the back, beating with the calf behind the supporting leg, and from there, it ends the movement by opening out into 2nd position. At the moment when the right leg strikes the left calf, the right heel skims the floor (the foot free); both legs should be equally and vigorously extended, up to the very top. One needs to feel the strike of the calf, and that the leg rebounds, like a spring, and, as a result of this tension, the leg cannot go further [across] than 3rd position. At all times, the leg never loses its direction, i.e., its full turn-out.

The movement must then be repeated, beating first in back and then in front, before opening to 2nd position. The number of changes of the feet can be increased, depending on which step one intends to prepare. To prepare for assemblé battu, one change is enough, while for the entrechats: two or more. Regarding the execution of the classical *pas*, we must remember that these are all done with the toes extended and the arches lifted (except for the aforementioned), and that whenever we speak of the toes being extended, it is intended, without mentioning it each time, to include the lifted arch; for it is impossible to extend the toes without involving the lifting action of the arches.

GRANDS BATTEMENTS JETÉS[2]

These are executed like battements tendus, except that the leg continues the movement and is thrown forcefully to a height of 90°.

The body should neither make any involuntary movements, nor flinch, [which can] occur from misguided efforts. The body remains quiet, while the leg works independently, without involving other muscles in the movement. "Don't help with the upper body!" the teacher exclaims. "No sinking in the other leg!" An inexperienced dancer tenses the shoulders, neck and arms. The hand that lies on the barre, with elbow lowered, should not change its position; the barre is only a point of support, and the dancer should not grip it with force (fig's 11, 12).

A slight inclination of the body forward is recommended only when doing grand battement to the back, straightening it again with the return to 5th position, as only in this way does the line of movement remain calm and the leg work correctly.

In this exercise in the Italian School, the body is held straight in the battement to the back; but then the knee inevitably bends, and the entire line is broken and uneasy.

In the beginners' class, it is better not to demand that the leg be lifted beyond 90° in this exercise, so that the execution does

---

[2] When the name of a step or pose includes the term "grand" (big), it means that the leg rises to a height of 90°.

Fig. 11. Grand battement jeté front

Fig. 12. Grand battement jeté to the side in 2nd position

not suffer for a cheap effect. Therefore, the teacher should hold back even those students whose individual builds allow the easy raising of the leg to 135°. Only a mature and self-assured artist can to choose any desired height.

Grands Battements Jetés Pointés

This battement begins with a grand battement jeté, but the foot does not return to 5th position; the leg, with the knee and foot stretched, is lowered to the floor in the same position that is reached at the outermost point of a simple battement tendu. After touching this point lightly with the toes, the leg rises again and so continues the movement, returning to 5th position only at the last repetition. Naturally, the body behaves in this battement as it does in the preceding one (fig. 13).

Fig. 13. Grand battement jeté pointé

Grands Battements Jetés Balancés

This battement is done as part of the exercises at the barre.

To begin, take the leg to the back, the toes pointed; the foot then does a sliding movement through 1ˢᵗ position, and the leg is thrown to the front up to 90°, and, due to the force of this throw, the body inclines backward. The leg then rushes through 1ˢᵗ position and is thrown to the back, as the body inclines forward. The result is a swinging movement back and forth, and the body should incline forward and backward in equal measure, keeping the back straight and the shoulders absolutely even. The hand at the barre should not change places during the body's forward or backward movement.

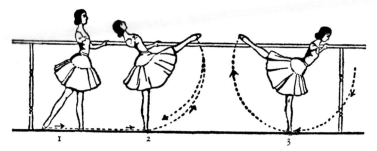

Fig. 14. Grand battement jeté balancé

Beginners are often satisfied with only the forward inclination of the body, avoiding the bend backward only because it is more difficult, which deprives the exercise of its form and sense (fig. 14).

Balancés can be done in 2nd position only *in the centre*, and this has a different look. Thrown to 2nd position, the leg then passes rapidly to 1st or 5th position and replaces the other leg, which is thrown to 2nd position, and as the legs quickly change, the body inclines each time toward the supporting leg.

BATTEMENTS FRAPPÉS

From the starting position with the right leg in 2nd position and the toes pointed, the right foot strikes the left leg sur le cou-de-pied front and returns to 2nd position, touching the floor firmly with pointed toes, the accent being in the 2nd position.

When doing battement frappé to the back, the foot does not strike sur le cou-de-pied, but instead passes behind the ankle[3]. This is the form for the initial studies of the movement (fig. 15).

In the more senior classes, when this battement is executed

Fig. 15. Battement frappé

---

[3] *Sur le cou-de-pied* front is the position of the foot on the ankle of the other foot, in which the sole wraps around the ankle, while the instep remains stretched and the toes pointing down. *Sur le cou-de-pied* back – the instep and toes are in the same position, but the heel is attached to the [other] ankle behind. In setting the position sur le cou-de-pied, one should pay attention from the very beginning that the foot does not assume a twisted position, and observe the rules described above.

on demi-pointe and the leg reaches 2nd position in the air at 45°, the same accent must be felt to the same point in 2nd position; the knee must be stretched and elastic, and the contact with the left leg must be a quick beat, the leg rebounding like a rubber ball. The upper part of the leg remains immobile and turned-out, and the leg must work without being shaken in the knee.

Battement Double Frappé

This movement is the same [as battement frappé], but the foot strikes once on the left leg front and is then transferred with a second beating movement to sur le cou-de-pied back, using the same technique as in the execution of petit battement sur le cou-de-pied; from here, it opens to the side (in 2nd position). If the first beat is back, the second beat is front.

PETITS BATTEMENTS SUR LE COU-DE-PIED

The starting position is with the foot sur le cou-de-pied. The foot opens toward 2nd position, but only half-way, as the leg does not extend at the knee. The foot then passes to the back, touching the left leg at the ankle, opens again in the same way and returns to the front.

Petits battements must be studied from the beginning at an absolutely uniform speed, with no accent.

At the moment when the foot is passing to the back or front, the rules already described for the position sur le cou-de-pied should be followed, i.e., the arch does not shorten and the sole of the foot does not bend. The upper part of the leg from the knee to the hip must remain strong, still and fully turned-out, while the lower leg does the movement freely.

At quicker tempi, the lateral opening of the leg becomes progressively smaller, but it must not disappear completely, transforming into a "smear". Although the passage from cou-de-pied front to back may seem nearly imperceptible to the eye, the movement must always be executed with precision and with the same clarity as when it is done at a slower tempo (fig. 16).

Fig. 16. Petit battement sur le cou-de-pied

BATTEMENTS BATTUS

The starting point is sur le cou-de-pied. From here, the right foot does a number of quick, short beats to the left heel, in the position sur le cou-de-pied. These little beats should be done with the toes, while the leg moves freely from the knee down.

This exercise is only done once the legs are well-developed. Practice is usually begun in the senior classes (fig. 17).

Fig. 17. Battement battu

BATTEMENTS FONDUS

From 5th position, the right foot is taken sur le cou-de-pied, while the left leg simultaneously does a demi-plié, keeping the knee turned-out; the right leg then opens to the front, with the toes pointed to the floor, while the left leg extends, the knee straightening at the same time as the right. The right foot returns sur le cou-de-pied, and the movement is repeated in 2nd position and to the back, and in the latter case, the foot passes sur le cou-de-pied back.

Attention must be paid in this battement that neither is the knee lifted, nor the leg raised, which are only applied when the exercise is executed with the leg at a 45° or 90° angle (fig. 18).

1   2   3

Fig. 18. Battement fondu

One must also take care in both big and small développés that the legs are turned-out as carefully as in battement tendu – for example, in doing this movement to the back, make sure that the knee is not allowed to drop and that the upper part of the leg is well supported.

This movement belongs in the category of more complicated exercises, because the standing leg also participates in the work, doing plié simultaneously to the battement of the other leg.

BATTEMENTS SOUTENUS

From 5th position, while the right leg is taken out either to the front, to 2nd position or to the back, the left leg does a plié; then, rising to demi-pointe on the left foot, the right leg is simultaneously drawn in to the left, and the two stretched legs meet together in 5th position on demi-pointe. From here, the movement can be repeated or done to the other side (fig. 19). The working leg must neither bend, nor be raised too high (when the movement is done on the floor and not at an angle of 45° or 90°).

Fig. 19. Battement soutenu

BATTEMENTS DÉVELOPPÉS

From 5th position, the sole of the right foot, with the toes pointed, slides up the left leg to the knee, then opens to the desired direction, keeping the knee and heel turned-out. If the foot of the working leg does not reach the knee, the movement will look sloppy.

After the high point of the movement is attained (90°), the leg lowers into 5th position. When this movement is done to the back, the body inclines slightly forward, as in grands battements jetés to the back (fig. 20).

Battement développé is found in numerous variations within exercises. I will give a few examples:

1) With the working leg bent, so that the toes touch the supporting knee, the leg opens to any of the directions, before bending in again, and this movement is repeated many times;

2) With a small balancé and the extended leg lifted to 90°; these movements should be attempted with the toes only, so that the leg itself does not dip too low, but sways only slightly;

Fig. 20. Battement développé

3) The leg, extended forward, is taken with a quick movement to 2nd position, then taken again with an accent to the front, while remaining perfectly stretched, all in one count; the same movement is done to the back and from 2nd position to the front and back;

4) With turns of the body: do a développé front, turn en dedans on the supporting leg into 2nd arabesque, then return to the position with the leg in front, staying on the same leg and turning en dehors. To the back, the movement is executed as follows: développé back, turn en dehors on the supporting leg, taking the leg to the front, then return, turning en dedans. In 2nd position: do a développé to 2nd position, change legs quickly, while turning and opening the other leg to 2nd position; repeat the whole figure, and return to the initial position, opening the leg to 2nd position. The change of hands at the barre happens with the free hand taking the barre simultaneously to the turning of the body.

Développé is an adagio movement. A slow tempo is one of its basic characteristics, and it should be performed with a slight delay at the extreme points, especially in the lower grades.

The standing leg must be fully stretched, like a taut string, and the supporting knee fully turned-out. The arm at the barre should be free to bend at the elbow, above all when executing the movement to the front, where quite often the arm at the barre tenses, in order to provide support to the standing leg. This may make it easier to stand on the leg, but done in this way, the exercise loses its usefulness.

Of the many possible forms of développé, I shall now describe the two most difficult.

BATTEMENTS DÉVELOPPÉS TOMBÉS

This type of battement belongs to the small adagio. It is mostly done *in the centre*, although it may also be done at the barre. The movements are as follows.

Do a développé to the front with the right leg, rising to demi-pointe, and fall with the whole body onto the right foot into the deepest plié possible; the left leg is extended, with only the toes touching the floor; then transfer the weight back onto the left foot, lowering the heel to the floor, while, with a quick movement, the right leg repeats the développé, returning to the open position, with the left now again on demi-pointe (fig. 21). This battement is executed to the front, as well as to the side and back, and *in the centre* in the croisé, effacé and écarté directions.

In order to give the movement a wider scale, I always tell my girls to imagine throwing the leg over some object – this stops them from lowering themselves too early during the fall of the body, so that the battement becomes very wide, and the leg is thrown very far.

Fig. 21. Battements développés tombés

BATTEMENTS DIVISÉS EN QUARTS
(battements in quarters)

This exercise is practiced *in the centre*. It may be considered one of the first adagios. It consists of the following movements, which are executed either en dehors or en dedans.

From 5th position, développé to the front with the right leg, and plié on the left; move the right leg to 2nd position, and simultaneously turn the body one-quarter of a turn en dehors on demi-pointe; bend the right leg in to touch the left knee, and, without lowering into 5th position, repeat the movement again (fig. 22).

one   [preparation]

four   three   two

Fig. 22. Battements divisés en quarts en dehors (battements in quarters)

The movement is repeated four times, with a quarter-turn each time, thus completing one full turn (a full circle).

The difficulty of this exercise can be increased by doing half-turns each time, or even a full turn.

The arms accompany the movement as follows: in the développé front, the arms are brought to 1st position, and they open to 2nd position with the turning of the body. In the développé to the back, the arm movements are identical as for the front.

Then start with a développé to the back, doing the [turning] movements en dehors (fig. 23).

Both exercises can also be done turning en dedans.

1	2	3
	one	two

4	5
three	four

Fig. 23. Battements divisés en quarts en dehors (battements in quarters)

III. CIRCULAR MOVEMENTS OF THE LEGS

ROND DE JAMBE PAR TERRE

En dehors. This movement begins from 1st position. The leg is taken forward, just as in battement tendu; from here, the toes describe an arc through 2nd position, arriving at the back to a point opposite 1st position. From this point, the foot draws a straight line to the point where the arc was begun, passing through 1st position with the heel lowered to the floor and the knees stretched.

En dedans. This is the same movement in the opposite direction. The leg moves from 1st position to the back and draws the same arc and the same straight line, in the opposite direction, observing the same rules. The movement finishes with the leg closing in 5th position front, contrary to our general rule to finish such exercises in 5th position back.

When rond de jambe par terre is done in a quick tempo, the following préparation is used.

From 5th position, move the right leg to the front, doing a plié on the left leg, with the arm in 1st position; then take the right leg to 2nd position, straightening the left knee and opening the arm to 2nd position.

When done at a much faster tempo, and the foot no longer has the time to accurately do a full [half-]circle, one should aim to fully reach the end point with the foot all the way to the back in the en-dehors and fully to the end point in front in the en-dedans.

The leg often has a tendency to go astray and do the exact opposite – that is, in the en-dehors, to go from the 2nd position through 1st position to the front [without completing the half-circle] and in the en-dedans, from 2nd position through 1st position to the back. This makes the movement too easy and does not provide the necessary work to the muscles.

ROND DE JAMBE EN L'AIR

En dehors. From 5th position, the right leg is opened to 2nd position at 45°, with the foot pointed. From here, the toes describe an oval (elongated sideways from left to right), beginning with its backward arc. When the knee bends, the toes draw close to the calf (but not under the knee), and they should come neither in front of, nor behind the calf of the left leg. The hip joint remains motionless, as does the upper part of the leg, from the knee up.

En dedans. In the movement en dedans, the oval described by the foot begins with the forward section of the arc, and, in completing the movement, counter to the standard rules, the foot is lowered into 5th position front (fig. 24).

Once rond de jambe en l'air has been thoroughly mastered, and one moves on to a quicker tempo, careful attention must be paid to the pausing and fixing of the leg in 2nd position each time that it arrives there. For the préparation (preparatory movement), we use temps relevé.

Fig. 24. Rond de jambe par terre et en l'air

This is a very important movement that plays a most serious role in furthering the classical education of the body. It must be executed with precision and without the foot stirring up movement in the knee joint, otherwise the exercise will stripped of its benefit. Executed correctly, rond de jambe en l'air builds strength and stability in the upper part of the leg and properly prepares the lower leg, from the knee to the foot, for all of the rotary

movements, as, for example, in fouetté en tournant. It is especially important in this case, because any incorrect motion of the
leg can throw the dancer off her balance. Besides, a well-worked
lower leg (from the knee down), compliant and flexible, gives
expressiveness to all the movements of the legs in dance.

GRAND ROND DE JAMBE JETÉ

This exercise is done at the barre.

En dehors. In class, this rond de jambe is ordinarily preceded by
rond de jambe par terre, which gives the necessary impulse for the
more vigorous throw of the leg. From 4th position back with the
foot pointed, the leg is rushed forcefully to the front, passing
through 1st position, then it flies into the air in a half-bent position
at 45°, stretches out, describing an arc through 2nd position at an
angle of 90° to the back by rotating the femoral joint, and returns
to 4th position. The circle should be made as big as possible, as the
foot tries to cover the entire sphere of action available to it (fig. 25).

Fig. 25. Grand rond de jambe jeté

The leg must be made to work in a completely independent
manner, without involving the [rest of the] body in the movement. This is possible when the muscles are fully developed and
subordinate to one's will. In proper execution, the body remains
quiet, and all the work of the muscles is imperceptible, although
the leg – from the hip to the toes – does work intensely.

En dedans. This is the same movement in the opposite direction. One must take care that the leg, after passing through 1st position from 4th position front, is thrown to the back in an accurately half-bent position, solidly supported in the upper part of the leg, and from here, passes upward through 2nd position and continues its movement to the front, drawing a circle at a height of 90°. This gives power and widens the circumference of the entire circle described. It is necessary that the foot go precisely through 1st position before the thrust and not proceed [to full height] to the front in the execution of an en-dehors, or to the back in the execution of an en-dedans.

Grand rond de jambe jeté is purely an exercise movement. "Well-experienced" dancers will, on occasion, begin their class with this exercise, which prepares the body quickly for intensive work. However, students and amateurs should, of course, only approach grand rond de jambe jeté through the preparatory exercises, as the strain on the tendons and muscles of the hip is extreme.

IV. THE ARMS

POSITIONS OF THE ARMS

In the terminology of dance, I use only three arm positions. All other positions are variations of these initial three, and I believe it is unnecessary to introduce special names for these, especially as it is always necessary to show the arm movements, when it comes to teaching a dance or a complicated exercise in the classroom.

The initial position of the arms – a kind of préparation – is the preparatory position: the arms are held low; the hands are directed inward and are close to each other without touching; and the elbows are slightly rounded, so that the arm, from the elbow to the shoulder, neither touches the body, nor adjoins it under the arm. The manner of holding the hands in preparatory position, as well as in the subsequent positions, can only be illustrated clearly through live demonstration during the lesson. My method is difficult to describe in words. Some illustrations, however (fig. 26), will help to explain.

The fingers are all grouped freely, and the joints are soft; the thumb touches the middle finger; the hand is not broken at the

Preparatory position   1ˢᵗ position   2ⁿᵈ position   3ʳᵈ position

Fig. 26. Positions of the arms

wrist, but continues the general curved line of the whole arm from the shoulder.

If, at the beginning of training, the thumb is not held against the middle finger, as the attention is directed to the legs and body, and so on, during the exercise, the fingers will spread apart, and the hands will open. The tips of the pinkie and index finger should be slightly rounded; subsequently, one can deviate slightly from this grouped placement of the fingers, separating them in a natural way, free of tension, as though nature had compelled them to give lightness to the hands, and giving the hands an artistic coloring.

First Position. The arms are raised in front of the body at the level of the stomach. They should be slightly bent, so that when opening to 2nd position, they can extend freely and reveal their full length. In raising the arms to 1st position, they should be supported from the shoulder to the elbow by work of the muscles of the upper arm.

Second Position. The arms are open to the side and very slightly rounded at the elbow. The elbow should be well-supported with the same work of the muscles of the upper part of the arm. The shoulders should by no means be either drawn back or raised. The lower part of the arm, from the elbow to the wrist, is held at the same level as the elbow. The hand, which, due to this tension, tends to drop down and appear to hang, should be held up as well, so that it, too, participates in the movement. By holding the arms in this position during the lesson, we develop them in the best way for the dance. At first, it looks artificial, forced, but the results will appear later, so there is no need to worry. The elbow will never sag, and the arm will be light, responsive to any position of the body, lively, natural and highly expressive, which is to say, quite cultivated.

Third Position. The arms are raised, with the elbows rounded and the hands directed inward and close to each other, but without touching, and they should be visible without lifting the head. The movement of lowering the arms from 3rd position to preparatory position, passing through 2nd, should be done quite simply: the arm will come into the correct position by itself when reaching the final position at the bottom. One must be careful to avoid the wrong ways that are taught by some teachers, adding a cloying plasticity: in lowering the arms to 2nd position, they have them rise again slightly, with the palms turning downward, thus breaking the line. The movement appears broken, pointlessly complicated and sweetened. I repeat, the hand will turn by itself quite naturally when necessary. This artificial turning of the hands is a movement typical of those danseuses who define themselves as "Plastic". Their meager technique requires such ornamentation; otherwise they would have nothing upon which to build their "dances". It is clear that we have no need to resort to this in our school.

The position of the arms in *arabesque* is quite particular. Both arms – the one placed forward and the one opened to the side – have the hands extended, with the palms turned downward; do not overly extend the elbow or push the shoulder forward. The French manner of bending the wrist upward obscures the expression of the entire figure and places an emphasis on the arms, with the result that one looks at the arms and not the general line. My approach is closer to that of the Italian School, but the movement is freer, the fingers more relaxed, and the hand not so fully stretched out.

The proportions of the arms play a crucial role in our art form, and, unfortunately, correct arm proportions is a rare phenomenon. If you ask me, "What is more appropriate for our art form, short arms or long?" – I would choose the latter. With younger children, the movement sometimes seems sweet even if their arms are short, but as soon as the student grows up, dance movements require a much broader scale, and with shorter arms, the design of a dance is lost, and the full breadth of movement is missing.

PORT DE BRAS

Port de bras is the heart of the great science of the arms in classical dance. The arms, legs and body are educated separately through particular exercises, created for development of the leg muscles and the [correct] way of holding the body; but finding the correct positioning for the arms is what completes the artistic look of the dancer and gives full harmony to the dance, with the head providing the final touch that imparts beauty to the entire design and finishes the look. The turn of the head and direction of the eyes play decisive roles in the shape of every arabesque, attitude and all the other poses.

Port de bras is the most difficult part of the dance, demanding the greatest amount of work and care. The ability to control the arms immediately reveals good schooling. This is particularly difficult for those to whom nature has not bestowed beautiful arms; they must pay particular attention to the arms and, through careful control, can acquire a beauty of movement. I have had to deal with students who had naturally beautiful arms but no freedom of movement, due to their ignorance of port de bras, and only after having acquired this knowledge could they begin to cope with their arms.

It is necessary that the arms in preparatory position are rounded, so that the point of the elbow is invisible, otherwise the elbows will form angles that take away the soft lines that the arms should have. The hand should be aligned with the curve of the arm at the elbow; it should be supported and not bent too much, otherwise the line will be broken. Currently, there is [a trend toward] excessive extension of the hands, which produces a stiff, hard line. The elbows must be supported and the fingers grouped as previously described. The thumb should not protrude. Keep the shoulders down and stationary. The arm positions in port de bras must appear relaxed. Every movement of an arm (to a pose) should pass through 1st position. This principle should apply both to dance movements [performed] on the floor and to those in the air.

As soon as one begins to study port de bras, the performance of the steps takes on a more artistic and finished character. The hands are already beginning to "play".

If we require no more of the hand than a correct positioning in relation to the whole arm, while all our attention is focused on the development of the legs, no great harm will be done, because to accustom the arm to stillness, to independence and to freedom from the movements of the legs is the primary goal in the training of a dancer's arms. With children and beginners, the arms always tend to imitate the movement of the legs, to participate in the work: for example, in rond de jambe, the arms [inadvertently] describe the same sort of circle. But when, through hard work, the student manages to differentiate between the movements of the arms and those of the legs and feet, and sometimes with enormous effort to master the desired movement, manages to keep the arms quiet, not participating in the movement – that is already a step forward.

Besides, to develop the arms and take them to a state of harmonious obedience requires less time than is needed to develop the legs to the extent required of a classical dancer. The legs are developed, strengthened and disciplined through long and continuous daily work. It does not matter how little time remains for the arms; in contrast to the legs, they will get the necessary training anyway. One is reminded of those plastic dancers who manage in just a few months to nevertheless obtain tolerable arms, while one notices that their legs and bodies are still in a most primitive condition. Therefore, when doing exercises meant for developing the legs, the hand may remain still, so long as it is in the correct position. The hands come into play when port de bras is introduced into an exercise, giving coloration to it. This is also where the training for the control and correct placement of the head is begun, as it is the head that will determine all shading of the movement. In port de bras, the head always takes part.

The ports de bras are numerous and varied. There are no particular names for its different forms. Let me give you some examples.

1) Stand in 5th position croisée, right foot front. From preparatory position, the arms go into 1st position, are raised into 3rd position, then opened to 2nd position, and then lowered again – returning to their starting point in preparatory position. In order to lend to this exercise the character it requires, or as we say in class, "to breathe with the arms", they must be used as follows.

When the arms arrive in 2nd position, open the hands, taking a calm, deep, but not exaggerated breath (do not lift your shoulders!), turning the palms downwards, and with the exhalation, lower them smoothly, allowing the fingers to slightly and softly "lag behind", but not at all emphasizing this or breaking the wrist, and without exaggerating this movement.

The head inclines to the left as the arms reach 1ˢᵗ position, and the gaze follows the hand; when the arms are in 3ʳᵈ position, the head is straight, and when the arms open, the head turns and inclines to the right. The gaze follows the hands continuously. Thus, the facial muscles become accustomed to participating in movement. At the end of the movement, the head is straight front once more (see fig. 27).

one   two   *three*   four

Fig. 27. Port de bras *(first)*

2) Stand in 5ᵗʰ position, right foot front. From preparatory position, the arms go into 1ˢᵗ position, then the left arm goes to 3ʳᵈ position and the right to 2ⁿᵈ position; the left then goes to 2ⁿᵈ and the right to 3ʳᵈ; the left is then lowered to preparatory position, which it passes through to rise again to 1ˢᵗ, where it meets the descending right arm. From here, the entire movement is repeated.

upbeat   *one*   *two*   *three*

Fig. 28. Port de bras *(second)*

The head accompanies as follows: when the arms are in 1st position, look at the hands, having inclined the head to the left; in the next position, the head is turned to the right; when the right arm is in 3rd position, the head is inclined and turned to the left; at the movement's finish, the head is turned to the left (fig. 28).

3) Stand in 5th position. Open the arms into 2nd position (head to the right), let them "breathe", as described in the first port de bras, and lower them to preparatory position, simultaneously inclining the body and head forward, [while] maintaining the symmetry [lit.: harmony] of the back by supporting the spine. From there, the extension begins, as follows: first, the body straightens up, i.e., it rises upward (returns), the head and torso rising together with the arms, which pass through 1st and on to 3rd position; from here, the body bends as far backward as possible, without throwing the head back; the arms, according to the rules already established, should be held in front of the head, and the gaze is directed at them; then the body unbends, the entire figure straightening, and the arms open to 2nd position.

one   two   three

four

Fig. 29. Port de bras (*third*)

The study of this port de bras may be done in 4/4 time: on *one* – bend the body forward, on *two* – return to the normal upright position, on *three* – bend backward, and on *four* – return to the normal position and open the arms to 2nd position (fig. 29).

4) This exercise belongs to the Italian School; but it is also widely practiced by us and is applied in all exercises. However, for this port de bras to bear the full imprint of the artistry that, despite its apparent simplicity, is inherent to it, it must be refined with great care. I will try to describe it in detail, although it is difficult to express in words the free, smooth flowing of its intertwined elements.

Stand in 5th position, right foot front. The arms pass through 1st position, the left going on to 3rd position and the right to 2nd (préparation for this type of port de bras). Open the left arm to 2nd position, and at the same time, after curving the spine inward, open the chest strongly, while holding the back and arching the spine, taking the left shoulder far enough *to the back* to see it well behind in the mirror, and, as you are turned to the left, the right shoulder will be *forward*, the head turned to the right. Despite the strong rotation of the torso, the feet remain absolutely still. Then the right arm moves to 1st position, where the left arm, rising from below, meets it. The gaze remains on the hands, with the head rotated to the left. The body returns to the initial position.

Now, let's look at the details. When the left arm is in 3rd position and the right in 2nd position, and the head is turned to the right, to take the arms into the indicated pose, lift the hands and turn the head toward the left arm (lifting the gaze); one needs to sustain this specified position, [then] having turned the palms downward and extended the fingers, do as if cutting the air and meeting resistance, so that the wrists bend slightly and the hands lag slightly behind.

When both arms reach 2nd position and the body is completely turned as required, the arms relax at the elbow, enough to drop slightly, seeming soft and effortless, like "fins". All this comes out of the arched back, which gives this exercise its finished, artistic and non-scholastic aspect. When the body is straightened out, the head is directed over the right shoulder (fig. 30).

I	2	3	4	5
upbeat	one	two	three	four

Fig. 30. Port de bras (*fourth*)

5) This port de bras is usually done at the end of the lesson, when the body is warm; it helps to develop greater flexibility. Stand in 5th position, right leg front, with the left arm raised in 3rd position and the right extended in 2nd position; incline the body forward (together with the head, which is turned toward the left arm), without losing the straightness of the spine; the left arm is lowered to 1st position, and the right arm, after having passed through preparatory position, meets it in 1st position; the body then bends back, with a rotation to the left, the gaze following the movement of the arms the entire time. The arms move from 1st position like this: the right lifts to 3rd position, and the left opens into 2nd, the head and gaze following the left arm (as the left shoulder pulls away, take care not to raise the right shoulder). The body then comes back to its starting position, the right arm opening to 2nd position and the left arm rising to 3rd position (fig. 31).

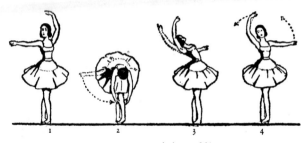

1	2	3	4

Fig. 31. Port de bras (*fifth*)

6) *Grand port de bras.* Stand in the croisée back pose with the left leg behind (the left arm is already in 3rd position, the right in 2nd). Plié on the right leg, sliding the left foot to the back; at the same time, lean the body forward, along with the left arm, without losing its position in 3rd. When inclining the torso as far forward as possible, the back should be held perfectly straight, not allowing it to curve or stoop. In order not to lose the symmetry, it is necessary, despite the strong inclination forward, to hold the spine perfectly straight, avoiding any hint of rounding in the shoulders, and during this time, the right arm goes down and meets the left in 1st position, maintaining its correct position in front of the diaphragm. Having reached a very wide 4th position – as wide as your body allows – straighten the body up, simultaneously shifting the weight back onto the toes of the left foot. Bend well back, using the muscles of the back to their greatest extent. The right arm goes to 3rd position and the left to 2nd (the right arm always stays in front of the head!). The head is thrown back over the left shoulder, similar to the pose in the 4th port de bras, i.e., with the left shoulder taken well back. Then the right arm opens into 2nd position, the head turns to the right, the body straightens up, and the left arm goes to 3rd position, and return through [4th position] plié to the starting pose croisée (fig. 32).

Fig. 32. Grand port de bras (*sixth*)

This port de bras is often done in adagio as a preparation for big pirouettes. In this case, as the movement itself is not carried through to the end, you stay on the bent right leg in a wide 4th position, with the right arm in 3rd position and the left in 2nd position.

To prepare for a pirouette en dehors, the left arm then rises from 2nd position, passes through 3rd and finishes in front in the pose préparation à la pirouette, while the right arm opens to 2nd position. For a pirouette en dedans, [after] the arms have reached the same position, the right arm is then brought with a wide, circular movement into a rounded 1st position, leaving the left arm extended in 2nd position. From here, the pirouette begins.

These last two types of port de bras are very important in our training. A dancer who has understood them can be considered to have attained coordination between the body, head and arms, and has taken a big step in mastering the play of the body.

I shall not continue with [other] examples of port de bras – they can be varied infinitely by combining the basic elements.

Some remarks on the work of the arms.

If you have done, for example, a développé into 2nd position at 90° with the arms in 2nd position, you must lower the arms first, the extended leg not moving until the arms have begun to move; the lowering of the leg still finishes simultaneously with the arms. This gives firm control of the leg, and the entire movement will take on a calm, unhurried aspect.

When executing the small danced movements of adagio or allegro, i.e., those with small poses, the arms are not lifted high. They only attain their full height in the big poses. This should be taken into consideration when doing small adagio or allegro exercises, so that the play of the arms does not overshadow the movements of the legs.

EXAMPLES OF THE USE
OF THE ARMS IN EXERCISES

When a complicated combination with various figures and steps is given, the arms start to take part in the general movement and play a significant role. For example, there are many different figures for développé, and in all of them, the arms participate in the movement.

Examples of Exercises at the Barre

1) Three ronds de jambe [en l'air] en dehors in three half-beats [lit.: 3/8] with a stop on the fourth half-beat [lit.: eighth] in plié on the left leg in a pose effacée front, [toes] to the floor, turning the entire body and bending toward the leg, together with the arm. Extend the fingers, as if pointing to the tips of the toes. Then do three battements frappés in three half-beats, with a stop on the fourth half-beat in 2nd position. Three ronds de jambe en l'air en dedans, stopping in the pose effacée back, toes to the floor, in plié on the left leg. The body bends to the back, with the head turned to look over the shoulder toward the toes, the arm extended in front of the chest, palm down, and the hand outstretched and lifted. Finish with three battements frappés in the same tempo as before, i.e., with a stop on the fourth half-beat in 2nd position.

2) Six petits battements in three beats (one half-beat each) [lit.: in 3/4 (each 1/8)]; on the fourth beat, fall into plié on the right leg (changing legs) in a small pose croisée, with the right arm closed and the left foot sur le cou-de-pied back; then change back onto the left foot, and do four petits battements in two beats, one half-beat each, and in two beats, do a turn en dehors sur le cou-de-pied from a préparation temps relevé.

All these movements are [then] done in reverse using the same counts, but after the first six petits battements, the fall into plié goes onto the right foot back, replacing the left foot, which must go sur le cou-de-pied front in a small pose croisée, the right arm opening slightly to 2nd position at 45°; after the next four petits battements, temps relevé is done to the back, and the turn is en dedans.

Temps lié (*in the centre*)

This is a combination of movements, already standard in the elementary grades, that gradually increases in difficulty. The simplest [form of] temps lié is performed as follows:

Stand in 5th position croisée, right foot front. Do a demi-plié, slide the right foot forward, with the toes pointed to the floor in croisé and the left leg remaining in demi-plié; both arms are in

1st position, and the gaze is on them. Keeping the head in that direction, transfer the weight onto the right leg, passing through 4th position demi-plié and extending the toes of the left foot to the back, with the left arm up and the right to the side. The head is now turned to the right. Close the left foot tightly into 5th position demi-plié en face, bringing the left arm to 1st position and leaving the right in 2nd position, with the head en face. Slide the right leg to 2nd position (opening the left arm to 2nd, accompanied by the head), staying in plié on the left leg; transfer the weight

| I | 2 | 3 | 4 | 5 | 6 |
| | one | two | | three | four |

| 10 | 9 | 8 | 7 |
| four | three | two | one |

Fig. 33. Temps lié

onto the right leg, passing through demi-plié, extending the toes of the left foot and then pulling it in front in 5th position. Lower the arms to preparatory position. Repeat the whole exercise with the left leg. The same movement is also done to the back.

I recommend that beginners study temps lié in 4/4 time, executing the entire movement in two measures: on the *first* beat, demi-plié in 5th position; on the *second* – extend the toes to the front in croisé; the transitional plié comes between the second and third beats; on the *third* – a pose croisée back; on the fourth – close into 5th position. Then move on to the next sequence: on the *first* beat – demi-plié in 5th position; on the *second* – the leg slides to the side in 2nd position with the foot pointed; on the *third* – extend the toes of the left foot, while transferring the weight over to the right leg; on the *fourth* – close into 5th position (fig. 33).

In the senior classes, temps lié can be done with the leg at 90° while moving forward, backward or to 2nd position. From 5th position, demi-plié on the left leg, do a développé croisé front with the right leg; transfer the weight onto the right leg in the pose attitude croisée back; having brought the left foot close to the right, fall into demi-plié on the left leg, bending the right leg in, at 90°, toes to the knee; do a développé with the right leg

one   two   one

two   and

Fig. 34. Temps lié (at 90°)

into 2nd position, and go to it, lifting the left leg to 2nd position at 90°; demi-plié on the right leg, bend the left knee in, toes to the right knee, and open it to the front to continue the movement with the other leg.

In intermediate and senior classes, temps lié can be studied en tournant: to begin, do a tour en dehors sur le cou-de-pied from 5th position, then do the temps lié to the front. Do the same tour once again, then temps lié toward 2nd position. In doing temps lié en tournant at 90°, after having done the tour, the foot is lifted to the front at the level of the knee. The arms are the same as when the step is done on the floor [without turning] (fig. 34).

In temps lié to the back, the tour is en dedans.

Temps lié sauté consists of a sequence of small sissonnes tombées, however this belongs to the allegro.

V. THE POSES OF CLASSICAL BALLET

ATTITUDES

The word attitude denotes the croisée and effacée poses on one leg, with the other raised to 90° to the back in a bent position. Therefore, a pose in développé front cannot be called attitude, because the leg is extended in a straight line. I do not call these poses other than développé in croisé or effacé. In attitude, the same arm as the raised leg is lifted, while the other arm is in 2nd position (fig. 35).

a	b	c	d
Attitude croisée	Développé front croisé	Développé front effacé	Attitude effacée

Fig. 35

The back leg should be well behind, and the knee should never be dropped. The leg being bent allows the body to bend as well, and so the movement in turns will be beautiful and easy, whereas the straight leg of an arabesque does not allow the body to bend and makes turning difficult. To better familiarize ourselves with the attitude, let us examine its execution in the French, Italian and Russian Schools, in croisé and effacé.

Attitude Croisée

Attitude croisée in the French School is taken with the body inclined toward the standing leg, so that the shoulder of the raised arm is much higher than the other.

In the Italian School, with the body and back both straight, the entire image is expressed by the turning of the head or by the raising of one arm or the other.

Such an attitude is wrong, because in this position of the body, the knee is poorly supported and hangs down – and if you support it from the upper leg, from the hip, the knee moves away from the body, and an ugly shape to the pose will result.

My attitude croisée is as follows: the shoulders are even, the body is bent back, [i.e.] with the spine not straight but curved, and the leg is taken strongly to the back; the head is turned distinctly toward the shoulder of the arm opened in 2nd position. In attitude, the torso inevitably inclines toward the standing leg, but owing to the position of the leg, the straight shoulders and well-arched back, the desired shape is achieved. The arms may be changed – lifted opposite to the leg – and in this case, the torso will incline to the other side, without spoiling the correctness of the pose. The direction of the head and eyes may also be changed, and with these, the facial expression; when the spine is working well, it is possible to manipulate the body as you like.

Attitude Effacée

If in attitude croisée, the leg is bent at the knee, with attitude effacée, it is only half-bent, otherwise the pose will be incorrect.

The Italian attitude effacée preserves the straight back, but all the same, the body crumples, bending toward the bent leg. In a pirouette, the pose goes off and the knee sags involuntarily, or, conversely, the knee lifts and the toes hang downward.

My attitude [effacée] comes nearer to the French. The torso is directed slightly forward toward the supporting leg; the arms and the entire pose aspire to the same direction, which gives this attitude an impression of flight. The difference with the French attitude is the same as in attitude croisée; despite the torso being directed toward the standing leg, neither shoulder is higher than the other. This attitude is extremely useful for turns (fig. 36).

I	2	3
French	Russian	Italian

Fig. 36. Attitudes effacées

ARABESQUES

Arabesque is one of the basic poses in classical ballet today. (If in attitude, the leg is fully or half-bent, in arabesque, it should always be fully extended.) The forms of arabesque vary ad infinitum. The four main arabesques used in our dancing are the following:

1ˢᵗ Arabesque (also called open – ouverte – or allongée, although at present, these terms are no longer in use). The body rests on one leg, the other being extended in a straight line and lifted from the floor, reaching a height of not less than 90°. The legs are in the position of effacé. The arm opposite to the raised leg is extended to the front, and the other is out to the side; the hands are extended, with the palms turned downward, as if to rest on the air. The body reaches forward. The head is in profile, as is the entire figure. The shoulders are level, as they are for all arabesques. In arabesque, the crucial role is played by the back, as only through placing it well is it possible to give the arabesque a beautiful line. To more clearly explain the correct position, let us analyze the French and Italian arabesques, as well as our own.

The French arabesque takes the pose languidly, with the body being held, but not extended, and passively inclined forward, and the arm is held artificially in 2nd position and therefore has a lifeless, inexpressive appearance.

The Italian arabesque eliminates the slackness of the pose; the body is held, but not inclined, the back being held upright, and the arm is taken sharply behind the 2nd position.

I specify the following arabesque: the torso is inclined forward, as if to feel a forward impulse, and the back is not languid, but rather arched vigorously and held firmly at the waist; the arm is opened comfortably enough to aid the muscular tension in the entire body, i.e., [only] slightly behind 2nd position (fig. 37).

1st Arabesque   2nd Arabesque

Fig. 37

2nd Arabesque. The body and legs are the same as in 1st arabesque, but the arm corresponding to the extended leg is taken forward. The other arm is taken far enough to the back so as to be visible behind the torso. The head is turned toward the audience (fig. 37).

3rd Arabesque. This arabesque is turned to face the audience. The leg is in croisé back at 90°. The torso is inclined forward, and the back is held. The arm extended to the front corresponds to the leg extended to the back, and the other one is opened to the side. The face is turned toward the front hand, as if the gaze is following the movement (fig. 38).

4th Arabesque. The legs are in the same position as in 3rd arabesque, but the arm opposite to the raised leg is taken forward, and the body is turned and held with a strong arching of the back. The other arm is visible behind the back. In this arabesque, the back is half-turned to face the audience. Make sure that the foot of the standing leg does not lose its turn-out. The head is turned to the audience, emphasizing the direction of the gaze. The shoulders should be level. The body should not lean forward. This is the most difficult of the arabesques, and its form requires careful study (fig. 38).

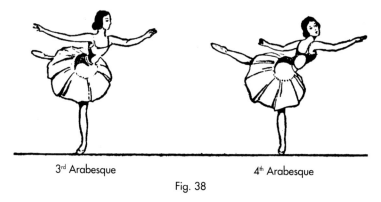

3rd Arabesque   4th Arabesque

Fig. 38

When we begin to practice tours in arabesque, the differences between the French and Italian arabesques and our own become especially clear.

When turning, the French arabesque makes it impossible to develop the movement, and in the Italian, the leg inevitably bends at the knee, breaking the line, which is constantly observed with Italians. The arabesque I propose gives stability and power while turning, without losing the extension of the pose and legs.

When doing a tour in arabesque, the arabesque should be expressed all at once; from the pose of préparation (4th position), having pushed from the floor with the heel of the front foot, it is necessary to pass at once into a sharp arabesque, otherwise the power will be lost, and the tour will not succeed. Being clearly conscious of this, one must "push off" into arabesque without expecting to correct the pose during the turn.

THE ÉCARTÉE POSE

The écartée pose is executed as follows.

Écartée back. Standing on the right leg, take the left leg with a développé to 90° in the direction of point *6* in our diagram (fig. 2b). The leg is strongly turned-out from the hip. The entire pose is taken on one plane, diagonally to the audience. Make sure that the foot of the supporting leg does not lose its turn-out. The left arm is raised in 3rd position; the right is in 2nd position. The torso should incline sideways toward the standing leg, but with a strongly-held back. [The pose] must remain natural, but not so simple as to appear inartistic. The head is turned to the right.

Écartée front – with the leg directed toward point *8* (fig. 2b) – is a proud and stately pose. The same arm and leg are raised. The head is turned to the same direction (fig. 39).

Fig. 39. Écartée back and écartée front

In both cases, it is [also] possible to raise both arms.

In essence, the écartée pose is a 2nd position développé, opened as widely as possible. In this pose, you need watch that, despite the body's inclination to the side, the shoulders remain aligned and that one shoulder is not above the other [i.e., not raised in respect to the line of inclination], which is [only] possible with a well-held lower back and waist.

VI. LINKING AND AUXILIARY MOVEMENTS

PAS DE BOURRÉE

In classical dance, in order to move from one place to another, one does not use an ordinary step, but rather a connecting dance step. One of the most common forms of such connecting steps is the pas de bourrée.

Pas de bourrée exists in many forms and is done in all possible directions.

For a long time, we kept the soft, un-emphasized figure of the pas de bourrée from the French School. With the increasing influence of the Italians at the end of the 19th century, the form of pas de bourrée changed. [Now] the foot is raised distinctly sur le cou-de-pied, and the entire movement is defined in higher relief. I chose this type of pas de bourrée, having tested it in practice.

One must take care that the foot is lifted distinctly from the floor, both in the early stages of study on demi-pointe and subsequently on pointe.

Pas de bourrée is divided into two basic forms: with a change of feet and without a change of feet. In the first case, if the right foot begins front, the left will finish front. In the second case, the right foot will remain front.

Pas de Bourrée (with a change of feet)

This form is used to familiarize elementary-grade students with the pas de bourrée.

Stand in the croisée pose, left foot back (the entire sole of the right foot on the floor). The arms are in preparatory position. Demi-plié on the right leg (the left foot goes sur le cou-de-pied back).

Step onto demi-pointe on the left foot, having brought it [close] to the right; lift the right foot sur le cou-de-pied front (but without pressing it to the left leg, keeping a small space between the two), change onto the right foot on demi-pointe toward 2nd position – without moving excessively from the spot; the left foot goes sur le cou-de-pied in the position described above. (This form is similar to sur le cou-de-pied, however the foot does not wrap around the ankle, though it can, conditionally, be named the same.) Fall onto the left foot to croisé in demi-plié. The right foot is sur le cou-de-pied back.

The arms assume a small pose croisée. Repeat the same with the other leg (moving to the other side) (fig. 40).

This is how the pas de bourrée en dehors is executed.

5	4	3	2	1
three	*two*	*one*	*upbeat*	

Fig. 40. Pas de bourrée (with a change of feet)

To go in the opposite direction, i.e., en dedans, to begin with, one must strike a pose croisée front with the left leg. Demi-plié on the right leg (the left foot going sur le cou-de-pied front), and step up onto demi-pointe on the left foot, bringing it close to the right; raise the right foot sur le cou-de-pied back, and change onto the right foot on demi-pointe to the side toward 2nd position, again without moving too far, the left foot going sur le cou-de-pied back, then fall into demi-plié on the left leg in croisé, with the right foot sur le cou-de-pied front.

The study of pas de bourrée can begin with a series of such

movements, making sure to pick up the feet precisely and extend the toes strongly. This will accustom the feet to pas de bourrée, so that when it is done at a faster tempo, they will not be lifeless, but will move with certainty, perhaps not so separately and distinctly as in the early studies, but nonetheless always participating in the movement.

Pas de Bourrée (without a change of feet)

This pas de bourrée is performed with an opening of the leg at the end of the *pas* and a step to the side. The same leg remains front as at the beginning, and care must be taken to not open the leg too far when taking the step to the side.

Stand in the croisée pose, left leg back. The arms are in preparatory position. Lift them ever so slightly to begin the movement, and return them again to this pose. Demi-plié on the right leg, then change onto the left foot on demi-pointe, lifting the right foot sur le cou-de-pied front (as in the preceding form of pas de bourrée). Change onto the right foot on demi-pointe, moving sideways to the right and bringing the left foot sur le cou-de-pied back; fall onto the left leg in demi-plié – the right opens to 2nd position at 45°, and the arms open to a low 2nd position (fig. 41).

To continue, rise onto the right leg, and repeat the same on the other side, to the left.

5	4	3	2	1
three	*two*	*one*		

Fig. 41. Pas de bourrée (without a change of feet)

I repeat: all these movements can be done in different directions: forward, back, in effacé, croisé and écarté, using the corresponding poses and arms.

If you perform a pas de bourrée without a change of feet in écarté, then, when doing the movement to the right, you will stop with the right leg in écarté front; conversely, when going in the other direction, to the left, the left leg will open to écarté back.

Pas de Bourrée Dessus-dessous

In translation, dessus means "over", meaning that at the beginning of the movement, the leg that is opened goes first to the front, replacing the other leg, while dessous means "under", and the leg opened at the beginning goes behind, replacing the other leg. One may further add that, in the first case, the one leg effectively goes over the other leg, and in this form, sur le cou-de-pied is behind the stepping leg each time. In the second case, the one leg goes under the other, and sur le cou-de-pied is in front of the stepping leg each time.

Pas de bourrée dessus-dessous, just as all the other forms of pas de bourrée, is taught first on demi-pointe.

1. *Dessus.* Stand in 5th position, right foot front. The arms are in preparatory position. Demi-plié on the right leg, open the left leg to 2nd position at 45° (having slightly opened the arms as well to 2nd at 45°), and, placing your left foot in front of the right foot[1], step up onto it on demi-pointe; the right foot is lifted sur le cou-de-pied back, just as in the previous cases; change onto the right foot on demi-pointe, having placed it in front of the left, which is lifted sur le cou-de-pied back; fall onto the left leg in demi-plié, the right leg opening to 2nd position at 45°. Do the entire movement to [i.e., beginning with] the right.

---

[1] Pay attention to not allowing the foot to move forward in a half-circle, but to cut a straight line [when] bringing it in from 2nd position to 5th. Through practicing this, you will avoid sloppy execution in the future. In the performance of pas de bourrée en tournant, this same detail of execution accustoms one, without thinking, to controlling the back, and then you will turn not quickly and without control, but with the proper delay.

Fig. 42. Pas de bourrée dessus on pointe

one   two   three

Fig. 43. Pas de bourrée dessous on pointe

The arms gradually come together in preparatory position and open to 2nd position at the end of the movement (fig. 42).

2. *Dessous.* 5th position, demi-plié on the left leg to open the right into 2nd position, and step onto the right foot on demi-pointe, the left going sur le cou-de-pied front; having placed the left foot behind the right, change up onto it on demi-pointe, the right going sur le cou-de-pied front, then fall onto the right leg in demi-plié, the left leg opening to 2nd position at 45°. Do the entire movement to [starting with] the left. The arms move as in the preceding case (fig. 43).

When first studying pas de bourrée, the accent [lit.: emphasis] is placed on the final plié. Subsequently, the movement will pass to a form without accent, the steps following one another.

Pas de Bourrée en Tournant

All these forms of pas de bourrée can be performed en tournant (turning). Let us examine, for example, the case that is often used in dance as a préparation.

Pas de bourrée en dedans. Start in 5th position, right leg front. Demi-plié on the right leg, the left going to 2nd position at 45°. Step up to half-pointe on the left foot, do a half-turn to the right, the right foot slipping quickly sur le cou-de-pied front; switch onto demi-pointe on the right foot, with the left foot sur le cou-de-pied back; drop onto the left foot in plié, right sur le cou-de-pied front (fig. 44).

5   4   3   2   1

three   *two*   *one*

Fig. 44. Pas de bourrée en tournant en dedans

From this movement, one can continue to pas de bourrée en dehors, as follows.

Demi-plié on the left leg, opening the right to 2nd position at 45°; step up onto half-pointe on the right foot, do a half-turn to the right, and slip the left foot sur le cou-de-pied back; finish the turn on the left foot, with the right sur le cou-de-pied front, and drop onto the right foot in plié, the left sur le cou-de-pied back.

Pas de bourrée, when performed en tournant, rotates around the body's axis, without swinging to any one side.

The arms open to 2nd position at 45° at the beginning of the movement, close into preparatory position during the pas de bourrée and open to the desired direction, depending on the step that follows (fig. 45).

The head stays directed toward the audience as long as possible, then follows the rotation of the body.

	one		two	three
1	2	3	4	5

Fig. 45. Pas de bourrée en tournant en dehors

PAS COURU

When many pas de bourrée are done consecutively, we get pas couru. It is usually performed at a fast pace. This *pas* is very often applied to running starts into big jumps – a jeté, for example – and is frequently found in men's dancing.

It is common in women's dancing on pointe, moving on the diagonal in a straight line or in a large circle around the stage. This is called pas de bourrée suivi.

COUPÉ

This is a small intermediary temps – a movement used to facilitate the beginning of other *pas*. Coupé is done as a preparation to gain impetus for the subsequent *pas* and is usually performed on the upbeat.

Suppose that we are given a pas ballonné to the front, from standing in the pose croisée back on the right leg.

We have to start with a demi-plié on the right leg (the left foot sur le cou-de-pied back) and then change onto the left leg in demi-plié with a quick movement, as if stamping the left foot.

The right foot goes sur le cou-de-pied and, from there, continues to move. Coupé back is done in the same way. Coupé can also be done in other forms, in accordance with the needs of the *pas* (see, for example, grand jeté, p. 129).

FLIC-FLAC

Flic-flac is used in exercises and adagios as a linking step between movements. In initial studies, it is joined together with other *pas* – for example, battement tendu.

Flic-flac en dehors is taught in the lower-level classes in a somewhat more simplified form than the one ultimately danced, in which it is a bridging or passing movement, so to speak. It is learned in two beats, as follows.

The leg is opened to 2nd position, and, starting from a low height (45°), the toes brush the floor, half-pointed, toward 5th position back, slipping beyond the sur le cou-de-pied back position, which happens inevitably owing to the whipping nature of the movement, [then] throw the foot out to 2nd position, and take it again front with a similar movement, passing beyond sur le cou-de-pied, and open the leg again to 2nd position (fig. 46).

Fig. 46. Flic-flac

In senior classes, flic-flac is done in one count. It should finish rising onto demi-pointe, or in a big or small pose.

Flic-flac en dedans is done in exactly the same way, with the only difference being that the foot passes first to the front, and then to the back. After this, we progress to flic-flac en tournant.

Flic-flac en Tournant

En dehors. Start with the leg and arms open in 2nd position. In the first movement, the arms meet together in a low position, in order to give a pushing impulse that will turn the body en dehors. In the second movement, after the foot comes front, the required pose is taken. The first movement is done en face, and the second is done in the turn (rising to demi-pointe during the turn and remaining so in the final pose).

En dedans. The reverse is done. The first foot movement is to the front, and the body turns en dedans. Finish in the required pose.

Flic-flac may be used as an in-between movement in adagio and also in combined exercises, not [only] from 2nd position, but from any other position. The first movement should be performed in the same direction where the foot is in the given instance, without letting it go to 2nd position.

PASSÉ

Passé corresponds to its French name – passing or transferring. For us, it serves as an auxiliary movement for transferring the leg from one position to another.

If we stand in développé effacé front and want to take the leg to arabesque without doing a grand rond de jambe, we bend the knee, leaving the thigh at 90° and keeping the toes close to the standing leg, then place the leg in 3rd arabesque. This passage of the foot is called passé.

The same movement can be done with a jump, leaving the floor with the standing leg. This too is called passé.

Passé can also be done on the floor, as in rond de jambe par terre, where it will be passé through 1st position.

TEMPS RELEVÉ

The French name of this movement comes from the verb *se relever* (to raise oneself), and this determines its shape. It is often used as a preparation for another step, and it takes a particular form when used as a preparation for a turn. We will describe that later and start with the basic forms – petit and grand [temps] relevé.

Petit Temps Relevé

Stand in 5th position, right leg front. Do a demi-plié, taking the right foot sur le cou-de-pied front, as shown in figure 47. The right arm is closed into 1st position, the right leg is taken with a passing movement forward and, without stopping, it opens to 2nd position at 45°, while the right arm simultaneously opens to 2nd position and we rise to demi-pointe on the left leg. When beginning this movement, the upper part of the leg (from the knee up) must remain motionless, and the passing movement to 2nd position must be done with the lower part of the leg only (from the knee down), keeping the upper part of the leg from changing position. Thus, the lower leg moves to the front only as much as the control of the thigh muscles allows. Temps relevé to the back is done in the same way, starting sur le cou-de-pied back, i.e., the passing movement is done to the back, bringing the leg into 2nd position, all while holding the upper part of the leg, which is to say, trying to do the movement with the lower part of the leg, from the foot to the knee.

Here, the leg has found a new way of moving, one which we

Fig. 47. Temps relevé

have not yet discussed: this is a movement forward and back without moving the upper part of the leg. This will serve as the foundation for the study of tours executed from one leg, since such mobility of the lower leg allows it to work without involving the rest of the body in the movement.

Grand Temps Relevé

Start in the same way as for petit temps relevé, but the right leg is bent to a higher level, the toes going to the knee, and after the demi-plié, the leg is thrown to 2nd position at 90°, with the same control of the muscles in the upper part of the leg as in petit temps relevé and with the same passing movement, without any delay in the développé en avant. The rise to demi-pointe and the arm movements are the same as in petit temps relevé (fig. 48).

Fig. 48. Grand temps relevé

Temps relevé is used as a préparation for tours that are not taken from two legs – i.e., not from a preparation in 4th or 5th position, but from standing on one leg, with the other in the air. When using temps relevé as a preparation for tours, we do it in a different way: the right leg passes through 2nd position – without stopping and with a passing movement, as in its movement forward – and sur le cou-de-pied, all in one count, while remaining in plié. On the second count, the turn is done with the right foot touching sur le cou-de-pied on the left leg.

In performing tours with the leg in 2nd position at 90° using grand temps relevé, the form of the grand temps relevé does not change; the turn is simply added.

VII. JUMPS

Jumps in classical ballet are extremely varied in form. When analyzed, we can see that they are divided into two basic groups. In the first group are the jumps into the air – for such jumps, the dancer must give considerable force to the movement and hover in the air. In the second group are those movements that cannot be done without leaving the floor, but are not directed upward into the air; they are like crawling plants, skimming along the ground.

In this group of skimming parterre jumps are: pas glissade, pas de basque, and the first part of the movement in jeté en tournant.

The jumps in the air are, in turn, divided into four types:

1) Jumps from two feet to two feet, which are further divided into those that begin: a) directly from 5th position: changement de pied, échappé and soubresaut; b) with an initial opening from 5th position to the side and a final closing of the leg: assemblé, sissonne fermée, sissonne fondue, sissonne tombée, pas de chat, failli, chassé, cabriole fermée, jeté fermé fondu;

2) Jumps from two feet to one foot, which are [further] divided, as well, as follows: a) with both feet initially leaving the floor and finishing the movement on one foot (in a pose); included in this group are: sissonne ouverte, sissonne soubresaut, ballonné, ballotté, rond de jambe en l'air sauté; b) when the movement begins with an outward thrust of one leg (to take-off) and finishes with a landing on that same leg in a pose: jeté from 5th position, grand jeté from 5th position, jeté with a half-turn and emboîté;

3) Jumps from one foot to the other: jeté entrelacé, saut de basque, jeté passé and jeté in attitude (when taken from a préparation in 4th position croisée);

4) Combined jumps, in which the structure combines several

elements: jeté renversé, sissonne renversée, grand pas de basque, rond de jambe double [sauté], pas ciseaux, balancé, jeté en tournant and grand fouetté.

Jumps into the air can be either small or big, but no matter what the form, the gap between the dancer and the floor should always be visible.

In developing a jump, one should always follow these guidelines:

1. Every jump begins with a demi-plié. As the principal factor conferring force to the movement at the moment the dancer takes off from the floor is the sole of the foot, in order to develop the jump, it is necessary to pay particular attention to doing a correct demi-plié, i.e., not lifting the heels from the floor.

2. At the moment of the jump [i.e., take-off], if this is done from two legs, the knees, arches and toes must all be strongly stretched. If the jump is done onto one leg, the other takes the required pose, in which case, one must firmly observe that the upper part of the leg is fully turned-out, the back is straight, and the buttocks must not stick out.

3. At the end of the jump, the feet must touch the ground first with the toes, then [make] a seamless transition to the heel, lowering into demi-plié; and then straighten the knees.

As Volinsky correctly stated, [dance] elevation consists of two elements: the true elevation and ballon. In the strictest sense of the word, elevation is the lift away. One can leave the ground and jump high into the air, but this jump may be meaningless, simply a gymnastic feat. Any circus acrobat can jump over ten people in a row, amazing us with his agility, but one cannot acknowledge it as elevation of the classical sort; it is a mechanical trick made possible by well-trained muscles. In dance elevation, the jump must also take on ballon. The term ballon refers to the dancer's ability to hang in the air in a pose or position that is usually taken on the ground. The dancer remains in the air, as if suspended. And so, when we are dealing with a high jump combined with ballon, this is classical elevation. Elevation is developed through a number of movements: changement de pieds is used to develop the jumps that finish on two legs; pas ballonné is used to develop the "trampoline-like" jumps that travel forward, backward or sideways, and finish on one leg. These *pas* are a preparation for high elevation and must be executed with great perseverance and care during the third and fourth years of study and practiced in great numbers.

The study of jumps is approached gradually and from a certain [objective] distance. Children and beginners may begin with these exercises: stand in 1st position, demi-plié, surrendering the heels to the floor, and jump, extending the toes, arching the feet and extending the knees. As you land, the toes touch the floor first, [then] lower the heels into demi-plié, and finally, straighten up and stretch your knees. Jumping exercises of this type, starting at the barre, can be studied from the middle of the first year (fig. 49). The same thing is done from 2nd and 5th positions. These jumps are called temps levé. Afterward, one progresses to changement de pieds.

Fig. 49. Temps levé on two feet

Later, when temps levé is studied *in the centre*, it is often done on one leg only, i.e., jumping from one foot, while the other maintains the position taken before the jump.

CHANGEMENT DE PIEDS

Petit Changement de Pieds

Stand in 5th position, right foot front, demi-plié, push off from the floor and jump up, extending the toes, arching the feet and stretching the knees; as you land, change feet, so that the left is now in front. Land the same way: first with the toes and then with the heels, finishing the movement in demi-plié 5th position. This method develops soft and elastic jumps, eliminating any stiffness (fig. 50).

Fig. 50. Petit changement de pieds

For the more advanced dancer, I prefer another kind of petit changement. Everything is done as before, except that the toes do not leave the floor in the jump, but remain in constant contact with it, as if one were only rising to pointe. This movement is done in an uninterrupted series, without any pause in the plié, although it should be noted that the accent [lit.: emphasis] is not in the air, but down, into the plié.

The exercise becomes more energetic and effective this way, and it is done at the end of the exercises *in the centre* (after allegro) at a fast tempo.

Grand Changement de Pieds

For this exercise, the demi-plié has to be deeper and more powerful, in order to achieve a higher jump. Push the heels strongly into the floor[1], connect the legs together, with stretched

---

[1] The higher the jump, the deeper the initial demi-plié must be. Care must be taken that the strain on the heels does not cause them to lift from the floor.

knees, and try to keep this position as long as possible, changing the feet only at the last moment. Land in the same way as for petits changements. When changing the legs in the air, you should not open them too far, otherwise you will lose the form of changement de pieds, the purpose of which is to change feet in 5th position. The legs open as little as necessary, just enough to allow the change of feet – and no further (fig. 51b).

In the initial study of jumps, particular attention must be paid to the arms, which should remain absolutely relaxed, from the shoulder to the hand, and be slightly rounded, as in preparatory position; they must not jerk as if to assist the movement of the legs.

In the Italian School, a bending of the knees is used during changement de pieds (fig. 51a).

a) Italian   b) Russian

Fig. 51. Grand changement de pieds

PAS ÉCHAPPÉ

Petit Échappé

Demi-plié in 5th position, push off with the heels, and immediately, with stretched feet and knees in the jump, arrive in 2nd position demi-plié, adhering strictly to the rules for plié in 2nd position; return with the same type of jump, the feet and knees stretched, and finish in 5th position (fig. 52).

Fig. 52. Petit échappé

This *pas* can also be done to 4th position in croisé and effacé, with the arms taking the appropriate pose. In general, the arms should not be taken to high positions in small jumps like these. The high arm positions should be left for big jumps. In doing échappé, one must take care, especially in échappé to 4th position, that the [weight in] plié is equally distributed between both feet.

Échappé can also be done finishing on one foot. The entire *pas* is the same, only the ending is different: rather than both feet returning to 5th position, one foot goes sur le cou-de-pied front or back. This échappé is done in 2nd, as well as in 4th position.

Grand Échappé

In petit échappé, the legs open immediately into 2nd position in the jump, whereas in the grand échappé, after doing a deep demi-plié, the legs stretch in a closed 5th position during the jump, which must be as high as possible, and they open to 2nd position only upon the descent. One returns to 5th position with an equally high jump, forcefully pushing off from the floor with the heels (fig. 53).

This échappé can also finish on one leg, landing in attitude, arabesque or développé front at 90°, i.e., in any big pose.

Fig. 53. Grand échappé

PAS ASSEMBLÉ

Assemblé is the foundation for the development of jumps in general. For beginners, it is the solid base of dance and a first step towards it. Despite the fact that it is fairly complicated, assemblé is one of the first *pas* [taught to beginners]. It is introduced into the class exercises early, because if the students are able to understand it, all of the studies that follow will be easier for them.

Fig. 54. Assemblé

Stand in 5th position, right foot front, demi-plié, and with a sliding movement, open the left leg to the side, arriving in 2nd position with the foot pointed to the floor; with the right leg, which has remained in demi-plié, push away from the floor, the foot and knee extending; both legs then return simultaneously into 5th position, left foot front, in demi-plié (fig. 54).

From this plié, the movement is repeated with the other leg; thus, in performing this *pas*, one advances slightly forward.

One must pay attention to the accuracy of the 2nd position, i.e., that the foot does not deviate toward the écarté front or back. This accuracy during initial studies of the step will ensure correct execution later of its more difficult form, the grand [lit.: big] assemblé.

Assemblé to the back is executed as follows: from 5th position, right foot front, take the right foot out to 2nd position, and at the end, close it into 5th position back. This is how the elementary form of assemblé is taught (in two counts).

In the next, more complicated form, the leg goes out to the side with a passing movement (and without accent) to 2nd position at a height of 45°. This type of assemblé is done in one count. After this, the *grand* assemblé is studied.

In *grand* assemblé, when done [moving] to the back, the right leg is thrown out to 90° in 2nd position, as in a grand battement; the jump that follows – a big one – carries the dancer to the side. At this point, the left leg must be brought to the right leg, closing in front, and both legs are held closed in the air, landing simultaneously on both legs in 5th position demi-plié.

The Italians, in order to give the impression of greater height in the jump, bend the knees after the grand battement, before landing in 5th position. This bending of the knees in the jump lends a grotesque character to the dance and ruins the classical line (fig. 55).

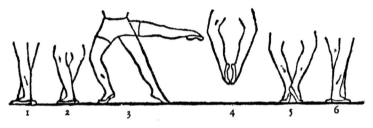

Fig. 55. Assemblé (Italian)

Grand assemblé is usually performed at a moment in the dance which is most triumphant. To have sufficient force for such a big movement, it is preceded most effectively by an auxiliary movement, such as glissade, or another préparation of the following type: do a grand développé en avant, fall onto that leg in plié, and push off forcefully from the floor, throwing the other leg to 2nd position at 90°; the push-off will be more energetic, and the whole movement gains in effect.

In general, in order to give emphasis to a jump and enhance its effect, it should be preceded and followed not by a movement of equal size and force, but rather by a smaller one. In this way, one movement will gain in effect from the other. In Don Quixote, for example, in the Dream Scene: the sequence of consecutive soubresauts and assemblés must be executed giving greater force and height to the soubresaut jump and, consequently, medium height to the assemblé that follows as a finishing movement. In this way, one emphasizes and gives brilliance to the first jump; however, one can also do the opposite, doing, for example, instead of soubresaut, a small failli, giving all the force to the assemblé itself.

In early studies of assemblé, I suggest that there be no participation of the arms, so that the students become used to holding the arms in a relaxed manner, so as to avoid both stiffness and jerking.

Once the students have mastered the assemblé, we can introduce the arm movements. The arms open to the side together with the opening of the leg to 2nd position, and they close again with the landing in 5th position, returning to preparatory position. Later, the head will also take part in the movement. When the arms and legs go to 2nd position, the head is held in profile to the side opposite the leg that opens, and at the finish of the assemblé, it turns to the other side, also in profile. I state that the head must be turned in profile, because an unclear turning movement of the head makes it seem as though it is inclining toward the shoulder, creating a soft, weak image.

In advanced classes, when one assemblé is performed immediately after the other, I do not require the participation of the arms. Only in the more advanced combinations, designed for already-finished dancers do I include arm movements in the assemblé. Assemblé can be done in all the directions: to the front, to the back, croisé, effacé, etc.

In class, you have to insist on a precise closing of the assemblé into 5ᵗʰ position. Sometimes it happens onstage that the execution of a step is not exactly as precise as it should be; to guard against this loss of precision, the dancer must exercise daily with great meticulousness and zeal, in order to preserve and maintain the level of dancing form. The more a dancer practices in class, the fewer errors she will make onstage. This is the purpose of the daily class.

PAS JETÉ

To introduce pas jeté, we use the following exercise.

Stand in 5ᵗʰ position, right foot front; do a demi-plié, and, with a sliding movement, simultaneously take the left leg out to 2ⁿᵈ position, the knee and foot stretching and the toes touching the floor in 2ⁿᵈ position. Then push off from the floor with the right foot in a jump, stretching the knees and feet; return the left foot to the place previously held by the right, and land on it in demi-plié, bringing the right foot sur le cou-de-pied back (fig. 56).

Fig. 56. Pas jeté

This is [how it is done] advancing forward. To do it to the back, the leg that is in front in the 5ᵗʰ position goes to the side. And the position sur le cou-de-pied is front.

Furthermore, jeté can be done in all directions, developing the style gradually, adding various small poses of the arms (and adopting the same head movements as in assemblé) and progressing to the study of jeté with the leg at 45° and to grand jeté in the big poses at 90°.

Here, it is appropriate to highlight the difference in approach in the Italian School to the jeté. In the Italian School, students are taught to throw the legs up very high and bend them sharply; the movement becomes strained, and its shape takes on a grotesque touch.

Grand Jeté

A big jeté, when executed onstage, requires an entirely different approach from a small one. Rather than starting from 5th position, it is preceded by a preliminary trampoline-like movement, a necessary transitional step before every big jump. The body needs to be sent forward, and it is necessary to push off from something. There are various methods to do just this: you can use pas glissade, coupé or pas couru, which already give the desired running start. Men often just take a big, messy run. I prefer a more complex approach that works the entire body and the arms, and from which the final pose arises as a logical inevitability. This is a coupé of the following type.

Stand in a pose croisée, right foot back. Transferring the weight forcefully onto the right leg, step forward to 4th position effacée, and, with a strong push into the floor, crouch down over this leg, bending the entire body forward over it, [then] push away from the floor, throwing the left leg up and forward in croisé at 90°, and jump up onto this leg, trying to stay in the air in a well-defined attitude or arabesque. The arms are used as follows: as the body inclines forcefully to the right, the arms are thrown to 2nd position; as the entire weight is transferred onto the right leg, the arms come together below in preparatory position, to lend, as it were, force to the jump. The required pose is attained with the arms passing through 1st position (fig. 57).

There exists, even if it is seldom used, a grand jeté to the back, which is executed as follows: left leg front in croisé, change the weight forcefully backward in effacé onto the left

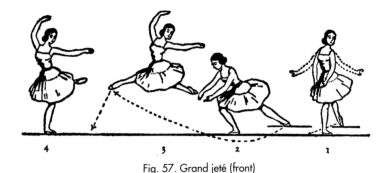

Fig. 57. Grand jeté (front)

foot in plié, and pushing off from the floor, throw the right leg to the back in croisé at 90°, jumping onto it and taking the pose développé front. The movement of the arms is the same as in grand jeté front (fig. 58).

Fig. 58. Grand jeté (back)

Jeté Fermé

Stand in 5th position, right foot front, demi-plié, and throw the left leg to the side in a 2nd position as high as possible, and jump onto this leg, transferring the entire body weight onto it. The right leg opens to 2nd position at the same height as the left. Land in plié, and close the right foot front into 5th position.

This step is done in two counts: plié on the upbeat; on the first count – transfer the weight onto the left leg in plié, dropping onto it; on the second count – the finish in 5th position. During the initial plié in 5th position, the arms are in preparatory position; from the moment the leg is thrown out to the side until the finish in 5th position, their movement is simultaneous to that of the legs, that is to say, they too open to 2nd position. The head also moves as do the legs, from right to left[2] (fig. 59).

This jeté is done forward, backward, in effacé, croisé and écarté. The arms follow the given pose.

Fig. 59. Jeté fermé

Jeté Traveling to the Side in Half-turns

Stand in 5th position, right leg front, demi-plié; take the right leg out to the side in 2nd position for a jeté (the right arm is in 1st position, the left in 2nd), change onto that foot with a jump, flying away toward that foot (to the right) as far as possible, and do a half-turn. Stop in demi-plié, back to the audience, with the left foot sur le cou-de-pied back, the left arm in 1st position and the right arm in 2nd position. The head is turned in profile toward the left shoulder.

Continuing the movement, take the left leg out to 2nd position, keeping the back to the audience, fly to the left in a jump, and do the half-turn just at the last moment in the air. Finish in demi-plié, with the right foot sur le cou-de-pied front. The left arm

---

[2] It is also possible to finish jeté fermé in other ways, e.g., with the leg carried softly downward. In this case, the movement is called jeté fondu ("melted").

accompanies the movement of the left leg, i.e., it opens to 2nd position, and at the end, the right arm closes into 1st position, and the head turns en face (fig. 60).

Thus, the first turn is en dedans, the second en dehors.

This jeté can also be done in the other direction, like this: stand in 5th position, left leg front; begin the movement with the right leg, turning en dehors (to the right [sic]) and finishing [facing] back, with the left foot sur le cou-de-pied front and the standing leg in demi-plié, the left arm in 1st position, the right in 2nd position and the head turned in profile toward the left shoulder.

From here, continue the movement to the left, with a turn en dedans, and finish with the right foot sur le cou-de-pied back. The right arm is in 1st position, the left in 2nd position and the

| 5 | 4 | 3 | 2 | 1 |
| two | | one | | upbeat |

Fig. 60. Jeté traveling to the side in half-turns

head en face. It is important to stay en face with the body until the moment of the turn, in the first case, and to transfer with the back to the audience in the second case. The head should be turned in profile.

Jeté Passé

Stand in a pose croisée, right foot back. Transfer onto the right foot in 4th position effacée front, in demi-plié, taking the body forward, extending the right arm forward in front of the body and keeping both shoulders level, i.e., without inclining the right shoulder toward the right leg. During the demi-plié, throw the left leg high to the back in effacé. With the jump, put the left foot in place of the right one, throwing the right leg into attitude croisée and arching the back (fig. 61).

Jeté passé to the back is done in the same way as the *pas* to the front: stand at the beginning in croisé, left foot front, change onto the left leg in demi-plié 4ᵗʰ position effacée back, bending

Fig. 61. Jeté passé (front)

the body over the leg, with both arms open to 2ⁿᵈ position, the palms open and keeping the shoulders level. Bend onto the left leg, throw the right leg high to the front, and with a jump, place it at the spot where the left leg was, and then, throwing the left leg up to 90° in croisé front, assume the required pose, i.e., the body and head can be turned either to the right or left, according to the direction in which the body turns (fig. 62).

Fig. 62. Jeté passé (back)

Jeté Renversé

From a demi-plié, throw the leg to the side with a grand battement to 2nd position at 90°, open the arms to 2nd position with the palms turned downward, jump onto the leg that was thrown into the air, taking the other to attitude croisée, land in plié, and do a renversé en dehors, finishing this in 5th position (fig. 63).

Fig. 63. Jeté renversé en dehors

The same movement can be done in reverse, i.e., after having thrown the leg to 2nd position, jump, and take the other leg to the front at 90° in croisé, and do the renversé en dedans.

Fig. 64. Jeté renversé en dedans

Be sure to finish the jump in attitude precisely in croisé and to execute the renversé correctly, i.e., avoiding that the *pas* causes the back to turn to the audience, which happens when, during the jump, the back turns too soon in the attitude or the reverse développé front pose described earlier (fig 64).

Also, do not rise to demi-pointe after the jeté, but connect it to the following moment in renversé, through the pas de bourrée, i.e., step up onto the other foot on demi-pointe, and complete the renversé.

Jeté Entrelacé (interlaced)

We begin the study of this step traveling from the front right corner of the stage (point *2*) to the back left corner (point *6*) on the diagonal (fig. 2b), so as to always stay facing toward the audience. It is easier to understand the step this way. Later, it can also be done in the opposite direction, starting upstage and traveling diagonally downstage; in this case, all the landings will effectively be facing away from the audience.

Stand in a pose effacée back, right foot front; demi-plié, lifting the left leg to 45° and inclining the body forward (left arm front, as for 2nd arabesque). Open the arms to 2nd position, and with a big step backward on the diagonal into demi-plié, change onto the left leg, and push off from the left foot, throwing the right leg to the front at 90° toward point *6* and bringing the arms together in 1st position, and after throwing the right leg into the air, jump up to it. In the jump, the legs seem to intertwine (this is

Fig. 65. Jeté entrelacé

why the *pas* is called entrelacé – which translates as "interlaced"), and only at this moment, turn the body at full speed, the arms throwing upward, i.e., hold the body en face as long as possible, so that the turn occurs during the jump. Finish in arabesque or attitude (fig. 65).

When the right leg is thrown into the air, be careful that it passes through 1st position, as this will help to preserve the interlacing of the legs in the air; also, try to land from the jump in the same place, otherwise the legs will be too far apart during the change, and the movement will lose its design. To keep the body from dragging and to help the movement, the arms must gain force in passing through 2nd position during the change onto the left leg – in this way, they can best help the entire movement.

Jeté en Tournant (par terre)

This jeté is given this name [par terre], because the thrust does not go upward, but rather horizontal, and its movement skims along the floor in a characteristically flat form.

Let us take as an example the jeté par terre that moves to the right on diagonal, starting from the back left corner (from point *6* to point *2*) (fig. 2b).

Stand in 5th position, right foot front, demi-plié; throw the right foot forward in effacé on diagonal with a movement that slides along the floor, drop onto it in demi-plié, pushing off with the left leg and throwing the right arm in the same direction –

Fig. 66. Jeté en tournant (par terre)

and the left out to 2nd position. The left leg rises off the floor as little as possible, no higher than 45°, and the whole figure takes on an elongated and stretched-out form typical of arabesque. Then, with a small, light jump, the left leg is drawn to the right one, the feet joining together in 5th position, and a full turn is done to the right. Land in demi-plié on the left foot, with the right foot sur le cou-de-pied front. This type of jeté is usually done several times in succession (fig. 66).

Jeté en Tournant

This begins with a preparatory movement. Stand in 5th position, right foot front. Do a small sissonne tombée with the right foot forward in 4th position croisée, into demi-plié on the right leg, then bring the left foot close behind the right, and transfer the weight onto this leg in demi-plié. With a sweeping movement, the right leg is thrown to the front at 90° and describes a circle in the air, while the body turns to the right. While turning, jump onto the right leg, and land in attitude croisée, resisting the force of the momentum and, at the same time, keeping the body from leaning too far to the right in the final attitude.

In order to gain as much force as possible in the sissonne tombée, the body needs to be strongly inclined forward; changing onto the left leg, the inclination goes to the left, turning the body to effacé, the head inclining to the same direction, and from here, describe the arc.

During the preparatory sissonne tombée, the right arm closes

Fig. 67. Jeté en tournant

into 1ˢᵗ position in front of the body, while the left arm opens to 2ⁿᵈ. When the body goes into demi-plié on the left leg, the arms come together in 1ˢᵗ position, in order to gather force for the jump.

The arms finish in attitude (fig. 67).

When jeté en tournant is done finishing in attitude effacée, the initial sissonne tombée is in effacé, and the final pose is in attitude effacée.

In men's dancing, jeté en tournant is quite often done circling the stage, and if the execution is not correct, there will be an excess of momentum during the jump. The result is a big effect, but, without the necessary emphasis on the fixing of the leg in the final attitude effacée pose, it becomes impossible for the dancer to control his body and finish properly.

SISSONNE

There are many types of sissonne. Let us examine here the following commonly used forms.

Sissonne Simple

The initial study of sissonne begins with the simplest form. From 5ᵗʰ position, demi-plié, and jump, keeping the legs together, with knees and feet stretched, as in every jump. At the end of the jump, land in demi-plié on one leg, with the other foot sur le cou-de-pied, and finish with an assemblé.

Sissonne Ouverte

Sissonne ouverte is a further development of the preceding movement, i.e., after jumping straight up, the leg, carried through sur le cou-de-pied, is opened to a pose at 45° in 2ⁿᵈ position, or to the front or back.

For [aiding] stability, beginners can be compelled to lower the leg after the jump, placing the toes on the floor in 2ⁿᵈ position, or to the front or back.

The arms take their position each time according to the pose specified.

In the more advanced classes, the jump will be higher and more powerful, and the leg is lifted to 90° in the pose attitude, arabesque, écarté front or back, etc. In studying [lit.: perfecting] sissonne ouverte, it may be done traveling to the side, or, if executed moving to the front, the pose will be back – in attitude or arabesque – whereas, in doing the jump to the back, the raised leg will assume a pose to the front – and in the écarté, jump to the side, and so on, in accordance with the direction of the desired pose (fig. 68).

Fig. 68. Sissonne ouverte en écarté a 90°

In intermediate and advanced classes, a more complex form is introduced, the sissonne ouverte en tournant, which is executed as follows: after doing a demi-plié, the right arm goes to 1st position and the left to 2nd position, in order to take force for the turn in the air, especially if there are to be two turns in the air. There is also another form of preparation: plié with the arms opening to the side in a 2nd position at 45° (to take force) and coming together in preparatory position during the turn in the air. Be careful not to take the right shoulder forward before the jump. Push off with your heels, jump up, then turn in the air, opening the leg while still in the air, and finish in the specified pose at 45° or 90°.

Sissonne Fermée

I will describe, as an example, [only] one form of sissonne fermée, as all the others are executed in the same manner, changing only the direction.

Fifth position, right leg front, demi-plié, and jump not up, but to the side; the entire body flies to the left in the air, the right leg opening to 2nd position.

When the left foot has touched the floor, the right foot closes together with it into 5th position back, the toe gliding along the floor. The jump is small, and the leg is not lifted high (fig. 69).

Fig. 69. Sissonne fermée

Sissonne Fondue

If we do a big jump with the legs at 90°, it is no longer a sissonne fermée, but a sissonne fondue. An opening at this height does not permit the right leg to close simultaneously with the left (as in sissonne fermée), and so, one leg assumes the character of a fondu, the toe not gliding over the floor, but the foot being placed softly on the floor in 5th position, holding it back slightly. The arms and head work according to the requirements of the pose. This is the form of the *pas* studied in the advanced classes.

Sissonne Tombée

Fifth position, right foot front, demi-plié, and jump from both feet into the air, with the right foot passing sur le cou-de-pied or at the knee, depending on whether the step is to be small or big. Land in plié on the left leg, the right leg opening immediately to the direction required – croisé or effacé – and then fall onto this leg in plié, as if it were an afterthought. If this movement precedes a big jump, as often occurs, especially in men's dancing, then the sissonne may be followed by a pas de bourrée, which is a very useful preparation for the subsequent jump (fig. 70).

5   4   3   2   1

Fig. 70. Sissonne tombée

Sissonne Renversée

First do a sissonne ouverte in attitude, then finish with a renversé en dehors. One should not to rise onto demi-pointe after the jump in attitude, but join this to the next movement, the renversé, through a pas de bourrée, i.e., step up onto the other foot on demi-pointe, and complete the renversé.

This can be performed in much the same way en dedans.

Sissonne Soubresaut

Sissonne soubresaut is executed like sissonne ouverte, but at the beginning of the jump, from the 5th position, both feet are held together, as in soubresaut, initially with a forward inclination of the body, and during the jump, it is strongly arched to the back. This must be executed very carefully, and, from the take-off, the legs must neither open, nor beat against each other, so as not to do some sort of cabriole from 5th position. It is very useful and effective to execute this step several times consecutively, on the diagonal in attitude effacée, adding – after the landing in attitude, with the right leg in plié – a coupé on the left leg and an assemblé with the right foot, flying in écarté toward the direction of point *2* (fig. 2b), as in the variation from the last act of "Don Quixote" (fig. 71).

Fig. 71. Sissonne soubresaut

SOUBRESAUT

Soubresaut is a jump from two feet to two feet.

Push off from the floor, and fly forward with the feet pointed, without opening the legs. Before the jump, the body inclines forward, and then, during the jump, it arches forcefully backward, so that the legs remain at the back. Take care not to commit the common error of joining the legs in such a way that they beat at the calves – otherwise you get some sort of cabriole, and many make this mistake.

To achieve the correct form, the legs must come together in the air not along their entire length, but rather, forcefully squeezing the lower part of the legs together.

Land on both feet simultaneously. The arms in soubresaut are given freedom, their position depending only upon the general style of the dance (fig. 72).

Fig. 72. Soubresaut

ROND DE JAMBE EN L'AIR SAUTÉ

Rond de jambe en l'air sauté is first studied as follows: after doing a sissonne ouverte to the side in 2nd position, do a rond de jambe en l'air, with a simultaneous jump on the supporting leg. A double rond de jambe is executed in the same way (fig. 73).

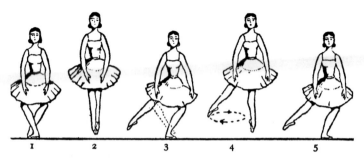

Fig. 73. Rond de jambe en l'air sauté

Fig. 74. Rond de jambe en l'air sauté

At a more advanced level, rond de jambe sauté is done jumping directly from demi-plié in 5th position (fig. 74). At the beginning, the movement is done opening the leg to 45°, and later, in the advanced classes, with the leg raised to 90°.

PAS DE CHAT

If we are standing in 5th position, left foot front, throw the right leg, half-bent, to the back in croisé at 45°, doing a demi-plié on the left leg at the same time, then jump off from the left leg, throwing it behind and half-bent in effacé to meet the right one; there should be a moment in the air in which the feet pass close to each other. Keeping the turn-out of the upper leg and without opening the legs too much, land with a soft flowing movement onto the right foot, and finish in 4th position, left foot front. It is also possible to finish in 5th position.

At first, the body should be inclined slightly forward, to enable it to bend further backward. At the moment when both feet are in the air, the entire body arches back, with the waist strongly concave.

This *pas* is refined by the positioning of the head, which can be held in various ways, as long as it follows the movement correctly.

The arms are hurled upward with a soft movement, the right to 2nd position, the left from preparatory position forward to a low

Fig. 75. Pas de chat

level. The hands drop down at first, and then are thrown upward. The character of the arm movements reflects that of the legs: the same soft energy justifying the name, "cat's step" (fig. 75).

The Italian pas de chat lacks this cat-like character: while the left leg is thrown in a similar manner, the right, which begins the movement, is thrown stiffly out to 2nd position, and the softness of the *pas* is generally not emphasized at all.

PAS DE BASQUE

This three-count movement is done as follows:

Stand in 5th position, right foot front. Demi-plié on the up-beat, raising the hands slightly up toward 2nd position before the beginning of the movement; the right foot slides forward in croisé and describes on the floor with the toe a semi-circle en dehors (the left leg remaining in plié). On *one*, without coming off the floor, jump onto the right leg into demi-plié (at this moment, the arms come together in preparatory position); on *two* – the left foot, having opened to 2nd position with the toes pointed, slides through 1st position to the front in croisé. On the *third* and last count, a jump is done, bringing both feet together in 5th position demi-plié. This jump stays very close to the floor, both feet sliding forward in the movement, the toes pointed, but without coming off the floor, and finishes in 5th position. This execution justifies the sense of [calling it] a *par terre* jump. On the *two*, the arms pass through 1st position, and on *three*, the hands open slightly. From here, the movement continues, the arms passing through 2nd position, and so on (fig. 76).

Fig. 76. Pas de basque

Pas de basque to the back is done in the same way. 5th position, right foot front, demi-plié, slide the left foot to the back, describe with the toe a semi-circle en dedans on the floor, and jump onto the left foot; the right foot slides backward through 1st position in croisé in demi-plié, and on *three*, the feet come together with the same sliding jump, but [traveling] backward. The arms move in the same way.

Grand Pas de Basque

In order to give more power to the jump, this *pas* is done with the arms thrown upward. To begin, throw the arms up into 2nd position, then lead them through the preparatory and 1st positions, and continue on into 3rd. The legs do all the movements in big poses. With the right foot, describe a big semi-circle en dehors at 90°, the left leg in demi-plié; carrying the right leg to 2nd position, do a big jump onto this leg (the arms in 3rd position), bend the left leg high, and throw it forward to 90°, opening the arms gradually into 2nd position. Lower the left foot to the floor, forward in croisé, and bring both feet together into the final pose, as in the small pas de basque. To give this *pas* a final polish, incline the head and body forward at the beginning of the *pas*, and return upright as the arms are thrown to 3rd position (fig. 77).

Fig. 77. Grand pas de basque

To the back. Circle the left leg en dedans, carrying it to 2nd position at 90°; jump onto the left foot, bending the right leg high and extending it to the back; fall back onto the right foot in croisé. The end of the movement and the arms are the same as for the front.

SAUT DE BASQUE

Stand in 5th position, right foot front. Without jumping, do a coupé with the right foot lifting to the knee, simultaneously surrendering the left heel into the floor (in demi-plié). Take the right leg a little to the side with a passing movement, and go onto it and, turning the back to the right, throw the left leg well to 2nd position at 90°, bringing it in during the jump (with stretched knees), the body transferring its weight onto that leg, so as not to stay in the same place, and traveling to the side in the direction to which the left leg was thrown. Then land in demi-plié on the left leg, while the right leg bends, finishing the movement by taking the pointed toes to the level of the knee. This bending of the knee is done immediately after the foot comes off the floor without any of the extra leg movements that are often seen when danced incorrectly. In this *pas*, both legs are strongly turned-out, especially the right, as its knee is taken sharply to the side.

The arms move in the following way: at the beginning, the right arm is closed in 1st position, the left is in 2nd; during the transfer of weight onto the right leg, the right arm goes to 2nd position together with the left leg, and the left arm, with a strong push, passes through preparatory position and on into 1st position, which gives force to this jump. At the moment of take-off, the left arm closes into 1st position, and the right is extended in 2nd.

On the return to the left leg, the arms also return to their starting position (fig. 78). During the thrust of the left leg, the head remains in profile toward the left shoulder, and it returns en face with the jump.

Fig. 78. Saut de basque

You can [also] cast the arms upward and into 3rd position; if, from their initial position, you lift them to the side at half-height, then, passing through preparatory and 1st positions, raise them together with the jump to give it a good lift.

When repeating the jump in succession, in such a case, the arms do not return to the initial position, separating instead to the side, from where, passing through preparatory position, they swing up again for the next jump.

There exists – even if it is hardly used in any dances – a saut de basque in the opposite direction, performed as follows: if, in the preceding description of saut de basque, one began by bending the leg [and placing the foot] in front of the knee of the supporting leg, and at the finish of the *pas*, the other leg replaced it, again [with the foot] in front of the knee, here, the legs move in the opposite direction: 5th position, right foot front; do a coupé with the left foot lifting behind the knee of the supporting leg and pressing the right heel into the floor in demi-plié, then, taking the left foot slightly to the side in a stepping movement, turn the back to the right, and jump, throwing the right leg carefully to 2nd position at 90°; bring it in during the jump (with stretched knees), transferring the weight onto the right leg and traveling in the same direction of the leg that was thrown, so as not to remain in place during the jump. Finish by landing on the right leg in demi-plié, bending the left leg [the foot going] behind the supporting knee.

GARGOUILLADE

This old French term has been retained in the Italian School. We call this *pas* rond de jambe double.

Stand in 5th position, right foot front. With the initial demi-plié, do a rond de jambe en l'air en dehors with the right leg; as soon as this movement is finished, with the leg open in 2nd position, transfer with a jump into demi-plié on the right leg; at this same moment, the left leg does a rond de jambe en l'air en dehors, beginning and ending at the right calf; after that, the left foot is carried to the front into croisé on the floor in demi-plié. This is how the step is studied initially. Its final form, as taught in the advanced classes, is more complex, in that the rond de jambe en l'air is done not in demi-plié, but in the air (fig. 79).

As this is generally a passing movement, the arms depend on the poses that precede and follow it.

This same *pas* in en dedans form is seldom used. It is done as follows: stand in 5th position, right foot front, begin with a rond de jambe en l'air en dedans with the left leg, transfer onto this leg with a jump into demi-plié, and do a rond de jambe en l'air en dedans with the right leg, beginning and ending at the calf, then open the leg to the back, following the same guidance given for en dehors.

Fig. 79. Gargouillade (rond de jambe double)

PAS CISEAUX

Stand in the pose croisée back, right foot back, plié on the left leg, and with a short and strong grand battement, throw the right leg to the front in effacé at 90°, throwing the body back, the left leg joining the right in the air, and, now extended, it passes again to the back, through 1ˢᵗ position on the floor to arrive in 1ˢᵗ arabesque, while landing from the jump in plié on the right leg. This moment when both legs are together in the air is characteristic [of this step]. The "change" of legs is done in a single count.

This is the form of pas ciseaux used for study; for the stage, there is another, more effective approach. When, after executing any given step, you have stopped in a croisée pose with the left leg front at 90°, you should do a coupé onto this leg, throwing the right leg into the air, etc. The body is involved in the movement, leaning very far back during the passing of the legs in the air, and is then thrust forward in the arabesque.

At the beginning, the arms are held in front of the body in 1ˢᵗ position, then they take an arabesque pose (fig. 80).

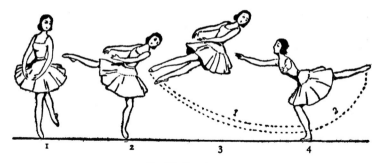

Fig. 80. Pas ciseaux

PAS BALLOTTÉ

This is a very difficult movement to execute in its correct form, and it demands a strength in the legs and body that is rarely possible for female dancers. Usually, they simplify it greatly and reduce it to a little jump with the legs going front and back, and above all, bending them underneath in [the shape of] a "ringlet", so much so that it deprives the ballotté of its original form. And in this case, the name of the step is figurative, evoking the image of a boat rocking on the waves. Indeed, a well-executed ballotté does resemble a rocking with the waves. There are no visible stops, and no pauses in its movement, as the dancer sways in the air, forward and back, with her legs closed and stretched, passing through a point that lies in the center of the movement, the body strongly inclining to the back, and then thrusting forward, which, with the legs stretched, effectively creates an image specifically reminiscent of a gentle rocking.

This sort of ballotté can be seen in Act 1 of *Giselle*, in the first meeting between Giselle and Albrecht; and it is often here that the more correct form of ballotté is seen, executed by the male dancer, who generally succeeds better in this *pas*, thanks to the strength in his legs and his suspension in the air.

Ballotté is done as follows:

Stand in the pose croisée back, right foot front. Demi-plié on the right leg, and jump, bringing the legs together in 5th position, shifting them forward in the air past the original point of take-off and inclining the body to the back (which greatly helps the movement); land in plié on the left leg, opening the right leg in effacé, then, without bending it, push off, again bringing the legs together in 5th position and leading them to the back past the original point of take-off, while the body inclines forward. Land on the right leg in demi-plié, with the left in effacé back at the necessary height.

The legs should have nearly no bending, and the body and legs should move as one. If the legs are well held, we will achieve the soft, wave-like rocking. The arms sway together with the legs. At the stop in the forward movement, the left arm closes in 1st position, and the right opens to 2nd position. At the stop on the right foot, the right arm is in 1st position and the left in 2nd position. The change of arms is done seamlessly and passes through their basic positions.

Fig. 81. Pas ballotté: 3, 2, 1 – front; 1, 2 and 3 – back

It is more practical to begin the study of ballotté from 5th position: do a demi-plié, bring the legs together in 5th position during the jump, tightly closing the feet, which are stretched from the beginning, and fly like this in the air, forward in respect to the point at which you were standing, and land on the left leg in demi-plié, with the right leg open in effacé front at 45° (fig. 81).

Finish with an assemblé. Ballotté to the back is done in the same way, i.e., after the jump from 5th position, fly with both feet in the air backward from the point where you were standing, land in plié on the right leg in effacé at 45°, and finish with an assemblé.

PAS BALLONNÉ

Stand in 5th position, right foot front, demi-plié; sliding the right foot to 2nd position at 45°, push off strongly from the floor with the left leg, jumping and stretching the toes so as to fly toward the toes of the right foot, [then] dropping on the left leg in demi-plié and bringing the right foot sur le cou-de-pied.

Often, when teaching this step to children, insufficient attention is paid to the accurate alignment of the foot sur le cou-de-pied; the foot passes too far over the other leg, the legs cross, and the resulting pose is wrong and ugly.

Fig. 82. Pas ballonné in effacé (front)

Ballonné can be done in all directions – effacé, croisé front and back, écarté front and back, matching the arms with the corresponding direction of the movement. For example, when we do ballonné in effacé with the right leg, you can put the left arm in 1st position and take the right arm to the side (fig. 82); but change the direction of the body even slightly, taking your right shoulder forward, and you get a jump in écarté form. Then it is more beautiful to close the right arm and open the left, slightly inclining the body back and to the left, as required in this pose.

One may also raise one or both arms to 3rd position.

In a big ballonné (at 90°), the leg may be bent so far that the foot comes up to the knee, but in a small ballonné, the more correct form is with the foot placed sur le cou-de-pied.

In performing ballonné, the body and arms should remain still in the same pose during the jump, avoiding strain and jerking in an alleged effort to help the jump.

When beginning to learn ballonné, it must be done it in place, without moving to one side: i.e., from 5th position, demi-plié, the right foot slides along the floor to the side into 2nd position at 45°, jump with the left leg, and close the right foot sur le cou-de-pied, with the left leg in demi-plié.

PAS CHASSÉ

This *pas* is seldom used in women's dancing and is more often done by men. It is usually done several times in succession.

Stand in 5th position, right foot front, demi-plié, and jump up, opening the right leg to 2nd position at 45° (sissonne tombée to the right), but with a more fluid movement than usual, then slide the left leg to the right, pulling them together; the two legs come together vertically in the air in a jump in 5th position, with the feet stretched and the toes touching. The jump should be executed moving in the same direction [as the sissonne tombée], and, as much as possible, be at its high point at this moment (fig. 83). This *pas* is performed in all the directions, and, as with many other steps, in the respective poses.

Fig. 83. Pas chassé

PAS GLISSADE

One would think that the name itself specifies the gliding character of this *pas*. In fact, we see that this step is usually executed carelessly (and smeared) and, in recent times, is being completely lost on stage. Particularly in men's dancing, it is often impossible to tell where they are doing a glissade and where it is a simple running start into a leap. This is a shame, because a well-executed glissade can help the jump, while a running start with the legs all over the place ruins the form and deprives a jump of its beauty and strength.

Glissade may be done with or without a change of feet. This latter form is used in the initial studies, and I will discuss that form here.

Stand in 5th position, right foot front, demi-plié, slide the right foot along the floor toward 2nd position, and extend it until the pointed toes reach 2nd position; without taking the toes off the floor, immediately transfer the body onto the right leg, then, without stopping, slide the left foot along the floor to close it into 5th position back, lowering into demi-plié (fig. 84).

Fig. 84. Pas glissade

This is the basic characteristic of glissade: that it begins and ends in plié. The ending plié promotes the subsequent jump, and because of this, glissade is the best preparation for jumps, replacing the running start.

Glissade can be done in various directions and in different poses.

It is wrong to do glissade like a jeté fermé, but it is also wrong to "creep", without coming away from the floor.

To avoid this kind of "creeping", the change from the right leg to the left must be done with a jump, but without taking the feet off the floor.

If you do a glissade as an auxiliary step to prepare for a big jump, you need to open your arms to the side at the same time as the opening of the legs in 2nd position, and then close them again into preparatory position; this gives good force for the subsequent jump.

PAS FAILLI

This movement is executed in one count; all the transitions are fused, inseparable, there is something fleeting in it, and it has its own peculiar charm and coloration.

Stand in 5th position, right foot front. Demi-plié, and jump straight up, with the feet held well together. During the jump, turn the body to effacé back, and slightly open the left leg – land

Fig. 85. Pas failli

in demi-plié on the right leg, with the left leg open to the back in effacé at 45°, and immediately, without stopping and with the toe on the floor, lead the left foot through 1st position, forward to croisé and into demi-plié.

However, the entire character of failli is obtained from the correct accompaniment of the arms, which do not need to accentuate the movement, but rather, to move softly, almost spontaneously. At the beginning of the movement, lift the arms slightly; then the left arm goes forward together with the left leg, while simultaneously inclining the body to the left.

One may also finish another way, taking the arms to the pose préparation à la pirouette, so that the final position of the failli can serve as a 4th position preparation for turns, or for any other movement (fig. 85).

PAS EMBOÎTÉ

Stand in 5th position, right foot front. Demi-plié, bending the right leg to the front at a height of 45°; jumping up, extend the right leg and land on it in demi-plié, having changed the left leg to the front in a bent position while in the air. Jump again, changing the bent right leg to the front while in the air. Finish in demi-plié on the left leg, with the right leg bent in front.

To do this movement correctly, the legs need to pass each other during the change, one after the other. Emboîté to the back is done in the same way.

Emboîté can also be done high, throwing the leg up to knee-level, but less bent. On stage, it is very effective to do a series of emboîtés, starting low with a very small one and gradually sending the leg higher each time – up to a grand emboîté at 90°.

Emboîté en Tournant

Stand in 5th position, right foot front. Demi-plié, jump side toward 2nd position, flying away with the entire body and the legs together, turning in the air and bending the left leg in front; land in demi-plié on the right leg, with the back to the audience and the left leg bent in front at a height of 45°; jump again, and turn in the air, flying away in the same direction and bending the right leg in front; finish in plié on the left leg, en face, and so on.

The arms should help. The right arm is in 1ˢᵗ position at the beginning and the left in 2ⁿᵈ; during the jump, throw the right arm to the side, and in the plié facing back, take the left arm to 1ˢᵗ position, together with the left leg; in the following turn and jump, take the right arm to the front, together with the right leg, and so on (fig. 86).

Fig. 86. Pas emboîté en tournant

PAS BALANCÉ

This is one of the simplest allegro *pas*, and can be easily performed even by children. In classical ballet, it is often used in a waltz tempo (fig. 87).

Stand in 5ᵗʰ position, right foot front. From demi-plié, do a small jeté with the right foot, moving sideways to the right, then closing the left foot sur le cou-de-pied back (on *one*); on *two* – step onto the left foot on demi-pointe, lifting the right heel off the floor and pointing the toes; on *three* – lower again into demi-plié on the right leg, lifting the left foot sur le cou-de-pied back. On each of the three counts in executing this *pas*, the body and head accompany the movement.

The next balancé will be to the left, i.e., jeté to the left, and so on.

5	4	3	2	1
three	two	one	(upbeat)	

Fig. 87. Pas balancé

CABRIOLE

Cabriole is done to the front, to the back, in croisé, effacé and écarté, in arabesque, from 5th position or from any preparatory *pas*: for instance, a small sissonne tombée or a coupé. The form of the cabriole remains the same, and therefore, I will describe that most commonly used: the cabriole in effacé front.

We start by doing cabriole at a fairly low height, and all the rules set out below for cabriole at 90° also apply to the study of it at 45°.

As in all our examples, we will do the cabriole with the right leg. To do a cabriole of the right leg, you begin with a préparation croisée, left leg front; from demi-plié on the left leg, the right leg is thrown upward to 90° in effacé front [together] with a jump; then the left leg draws up to the right and beats against it. The legs must be fully extended, with the knees well-straightened and the feet firmly stretched. The right leg must not be lowered to meet the left, which does the striking.

Land on the left leg in demi-plié, keeping the right leg in the requested pose – in this case, effacé front (fig. 88).

Cabriole fermée differs from that just described, in that the leg does not remain open, but closes into 5th position. The right leg must finish the movement at the same time as the left, in demi-plié in 5th position.

In both cabrioles, the body is in effacé, but it is more inclined than normal. When cabriole is done to the front, the body

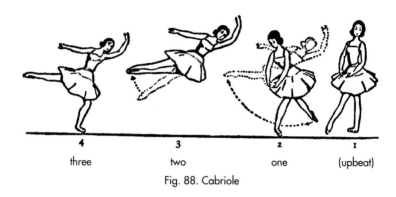

4	**3**	**2**	**I**
three	two	one	(upbeat)

Fig. 88. Cabriole

should be tilted back, while if the cabriole is done to the back in 3rd or 4th arabesque (which are easily taken from the same preparation), the body must incline further forward, i.e., in a position that is typical of these arabesques.

If cabriole is done in 2nd position or écarté with the right leg, you need to take the preparation with the left leg in croisé back and do a coupé with it.

In the final plié of the movement, the body needs to bend strongly to the left. This movement must be executed with care, to keep a correct and beautiful pose. The arms, in all cases, take the position required by the pose. For cabrioles in 1st and 2nd arabesque, it is convenient to take the preparation from a small sissonne tombée in the direction of the movement.

Cabriole is one of the most difficult forms of jump. At the beginning of its study, one can use the following method: open the right leg in effacé front at 45°, do a plié on the left leg, and, with a jump, throw the strongly extended left leg up to the right leg, and then land on the left leg in demi-plié. Repeat this several times, without changing position. Cabriole back is done in the same way, taking a small arabesque pose.

In men's dancing, the cabriole is beaten double – the calves beating against each other twice. Very strong dancers may even increase the number of beats, only that you need to make sure to open the legs clearly each time, otherwise the brilliant virtuosity of this difficult *pas* will be lost.

In general, the study of big cabrioles should only begin after the difficulties of the other jumps have been overcome; it is the most difficult and complicated jump, because it requires well developed elevation and ballon.

VIII. BEATS

In our practice, we often prefer to use the Russian word "beats" ["занозки" or "zhanoski"] over the French term "batteries". Because of this common practice, the Russian term will be used here.

A beat is a strike of one leg against the other. Beats bring virtuosity to the dance; therefore, their execution cannot suffer from carelessness, imprecision or simplification, otherwise they lose their sense. When doing beats, you must pay attention to the following rules. First of all, both beating legs must be well-stretched; and they should never beat with one leg being active *and the other leg passive*. Before every beat, one must not forget to open the legs slightly, in order to have a distinct beat. In the same way, when the beat is done from 5th position, one should open the legs slightly to the side at the beginning of the jump. If not, you get a smeared action, which turns a virtuosic step into some sort of nuisance.

If the beat begins with the legs open, i.e., not from 5th position, after hitting the calves, the legs must still be opened again slightly before closing into the final position.

Beats should not be simplified; on the contrary, to do them as much as possible in the most difficult form is a sign of good schooling. Small beats like royal, entrechat-trois, -quatre and -cinq, for example, must be done very close to the floor, crossing the legs very quickly in short, precise movements. It is much harder this way, but this gives more compactness, energy and brilliance. If these small beats are done with a big jump – high in the air – you have too much time to change the legs, and the performance loses its luster.

Beats are divided into three types: pas battus, entrechats and brisés.

PAS BATTUS

Pas battu is any *pas* in which one leg strikes the other. When one begins the study of the more difficult allegro *pas*, these can be executed with a beat – for example, in saut de basque, already very difficult, or jeté entrelacé with a beat, which only the men do, and so on. Let us examine a few examples.

To do an assemblé with the right leg with a beat, we proceed as follows: if the right leg opens from 5th position to the side, then on the return to 5th position, it beats in front of the left, then opens again slightly and ends in 5th position back. We must not forget to beat with the calves and then open the legs, before closing them into 5th position.

Jeté with the right leg with a beat is done as follows: the right leg is thrown out to 2nd position, it beats in front of the left, and in returning, opens slightly before landing in the demi-plié.

Petit échappé with the right leg with a beat: after the plié in 2nd position, on returning, beat with both legs stretched out, calf on calf, right leg in front, open the feet slightly, and land in 5th position with the right foot back.

Échappé battu can also be made more complex: at the beginning of the jump from 5th position, slightly open the legs, beat with the right leg front, and land in demi-plié 2nd position; jumping back to 5th position, beat once again with the right leg front, open the legs slightly and finish in 5th position with the right foot back.

This échappé can be complicated even further: before opening the legs into 2nd position, do an entrechat-quatre-type beat, and the same [again] when returning from 2nd position to 5th. With this type of échappé, it is necessary to do a big jump, almost as big as for the grand échappé, although I generally recommend a low jump for entrechat-quatre. But it is a difficult jump that requires more time in the air, and a small jump will not do.

This is how all these beats are done moving to the back; going forward, the legs do the opposite, i.e., beat the leg back, and finish with the final position being in front.

For the initial study of beats, it is better to start with the échappé beats before going on to assemblé and jeté.

ENTRECHATS

Royal

Stand in 5th position (right foot front), demi-plié, do a small jump, during which both legs are opened slightly, and, with the knees completely extended, beat the calves against one another (right leg front), open the legs slightly sideways again, and finish in 5th position demi-plié, having changed feet.

Entrechat-quatre

Fifth position, right leg front, demi-plié, do a small jump to open the legs slightly, and beat the right calf behind, against the left calf, open the legs a little to the side, and finish with the right leg front in 5th position demi-plié.

It takes the name entrechat quatre (four) due to the fact that the leg appears to pass through four segments of a broken line: 1st – opening; 2nd – beat behind; 3rd – opening; 4th – closing into 5th position.

I repeat, that all the brilliance of this *pas*, all of its essence, is in doing it as close to the floor as possible, with the legs opening and crossing clearly, so that one feels that the beats are done with both legs (fig. 89).

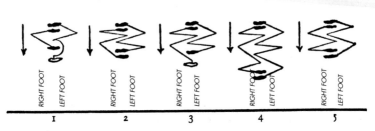

Fig. 89. 1 – entrechat-trois; 2 – entrechat-quatre; 3 – entrechat-cinq; 4 – entrechat-six; 5 – royal

Entrechat-six

Fifth position, right foot front, demi-plié, then jump, during which the legs open, the right beats back, the legs open again slightly to the side, then beat with the right leg front, open again slightly and finish in 5th position, with the right leg back.

The jump is a bit higher than the preceding one, but do not strive for height, because anybody will have enough time to do these crossings in a high jump, but the performance only shines with a low jump, as greater clarity and speed is required here.

Entrechat-huit

One more opening and closing is added; hence, the right leg finishes in front.

Entrechat-trois

Fifth position, right foot front, demi-plié, do a small jump, opening the legs slightly, then the right leg beats front, opens again and bends, [the foot going] sur le cou-de-pied back, while landing on the left leg in plié, i.e., this entrechat finishes on one foot, as do, in general, all those with odd numbers.

Entrechat-cinq

Fifth position, right foot front, demi-plié, do a small jump, during which the legs open slightly, the right leg beats behind, the legs again open again slightly, and the right closes in front, landing in demi-plié on the right leg, the left foot sur le cou-de-pied back.

Entrechat-sept

Fifth position, right foot front, demi-plié, do a jump to open the legs slightly, the right beats back, the legs open, the right beats front, the legs open again and then come together in the air (right back), and land on the left leg in plié, with the right leg in the air or sur le cou-de-pied, or in 2nd position at 45° or 90°, depending on what is required. The entrechats-trois and -cinq can also finish in various poses.

We finish entrechat-trois and entrechat-cinq with one foot sur le cou-de-pied back; it is, however, also possible to do them to sur le cou-de-pied front. In this case, if the right foot begins front, after the small jump, the legs open slightly, the left leg beats behind against the calf (the legs opening slightly) and goes to the front sur le cou-de-pied.

Entrechat-sept can also finish in other poses: to the front in effacé or croisé, or to the back in arabesque or attitude.

Entrechat de Volée

Entrechat can be done not only jumping in place, but also flying in any desired direction, that is, with the take-off. The most convenient way to do this is from a preliminary movement, such as glissade or coupé, but this step can also be taught from 5th position.

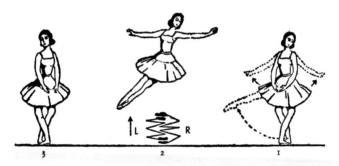

Fig. 90. Entrechat[-six] de volée

Entrechat-six de volée. 5th position, left foot front, demi-plié, throw the right leg out to the side to 2nd position at 90°, and jump, taking the whole body toward this leg and doing the beats of an entrechat-six. Finish in 5th position in demi-plié, right foot front (fig. 90).

Entrechat-huit de volée. Done in the same way, only the number of beats is increased accordingly.

The corresponding position of the arms and angle of the

head are the same as required for the croisée pose; if landing sur le cou-de-pied, the arms should not be high, one going to 1st position at 45°, the other to the same height, but in 2nd position; if one leg is raised to 90°, the arms should assume the pose for attitude, arabesque or to the front, or for 2nd position at 90°. In this case, one arm will be in 3rd position, the other in 2nd position, according to the pose required.

Brisé

There are two types of brisé: 1) finishing in 5th position, and 2) to one leg: dessus-dessous.

1) To begin the movement with the right leg, stand in 5th position with the left foot front, plié, and with a sliding movement, throw the right leg to the side no higher than 45° between points *2* and *3* (fig. 2b), then beat it in front of the left (both legs are stretched), which, with the jump, flies together with the body to meet the right leg in the place where the leg was thrown. Open the legs slightly, and finish in 5th position, right foot back, in demi-plié (fig. 91).

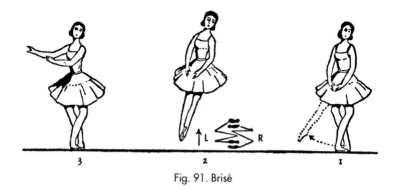

Fig. 91. Brisé

This step is often used in choreography. Brisé back is rarely used, but for the sake of completeness, I will describe this as well.

To move in the opposite direction, one must take a 5th position, left foot front, demi-plié, and slide the left leg back and to the side at 45° between points *6* and *7* of the studio, the left beating behind the right (the legs are stretched tautly) and flying away in the same direction to which the left leg was thrown. Open the legs slightly, and finish with the left foot front, demi-plié, maintaining the turn-out of the left leg.

It is important to be accurate in the direction between points *2* and *3* (fig. 2b) when moving forward, and between points *6* and *7* when moving to the back, in order to have a sharp brisé. Simply traveling on diagonal, the brisé will appear neglected and unfinished; the legs will not have time to beat properly, and the heels will knock against each other.

The arms in brisé take the following position: during the brisé, they open toward 2nd position, and at the end of the brisé front, the right arm is in 1st position, the left in 2nd position. The same rule applies when doing brisé back, only that the left arm finishes in 1st position and the right stays in 2nd. In both cases, the arms do not go above 45°.

2) Brisé dessus-dessous. This movement begins as follows: 5th position, left foot front, demi-plié, the right foot slides along the floor and is thrown to 2nd position, and beats in front of the left leg, then slightly open the legs to land in demi-plié on the right leg, the left going sur le cou-de-pied front (fig. 92).

Normally, this is followed immediately by a brisé dessous: the left leg opens to 2nd position, then beats the back of the right leg; open the legs and land in demi-plié on the left leg, having brought the right foot sur le cou-de-pied back (fig. 93). Brisé dessus travels forward; the dessous travels to the back.

In brisé, the body plays easily with the motion, in contrast to other forms of beats. Thus: during the brisé, the body bends forward and back in relation to the movement. In brisé dessus, the body must even bend toward the right side, and in brisé dessous, to the left, the head turning in the same direction.

The right arm is closed, the left is open to the side; at the moment of transition from one brisé to the other, the arms change – the right one opens, the left one closes, and the head is turned to the left.

Fig. 92. Brisé dessus

Fig. 93. Brisé dessous

IX. POINTE-WORK

Dancing on pointe, or on the toes, means, strictly speaking, to dance on the tips of the toes, with the arch of the foot extended. But pointe shoes are very diverse, and they depend on the structure of the dancer's foot. The foot best adapted to dancing on pointe is one with all the toes of equal length, as if "chopped off", with a low arch and a strong ankle. The same foot that we consider beautiful, with a high arch, a well-turned, slender ankle and properly-grouped toes, makes movements on pointe more difficult, especially the jumps on pointe that are now so widely used. If such a foot cannot be placed on all the toes evenly, as required by the rules of dance, it can still be helped, by diligently increasing the turn-out and trying to find support on as many toes as possible, rather than the entire weight resting on the big toe alone (fig. 94).

In pointe-work, the technique of the Italians has undeniable advantages. Cecchetti taught to rise onto pointe with a little spring, lifting distinctly off the floor. This manner develops a more elastic foot and accustoms the body to balancing on the pointe of one foot. The French way of rising smoothly onto pointe from the first steps of training eliminates the potential for

Fig. 94. Pointe

future technical perfection. A representative of the French School once tried to explain to us how to teach children to rise onto pointe at the barre in bare feet! Certainly the foot's strength cannot be developed in this way!

For a beginner, it is difficult to rise immediately onto pointe with a spring – for example, a spring up to 5th position on pointe. It might seem easier to rise onto pointe with a single move on [lit.: of] one foot – it comes easily; but this is inadvisable, because you must first, from the beginning, carefully learn to rise correctly onto pointe with both feet, in order to fully stabilize the foot ligaments; to approach this movement arbitrarily only pushes the student further away from a correct understanding.

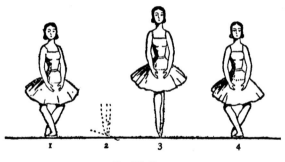

Fig. 95. Sus-sous

To initiate the first studies of pointe-work, one must begin at the barre. Face the barre, place both hands on it, the hands touching, and begin by rising onto pointe in all the positions, pushing the heels away from the floor before the beginning of the movement, being absolutely sure not to jump onto the toes until the ligaments of the sole of the foot have been strengthened.

Turning to the centre, stick to the following sequence:

1) *Temps levé on two feet.* Stand in 1st position, do a demi-plié, surrendering the heels to the floor, then a small jump onto pointe; lower into demi-plié, keeping full turn-out, and continue.

The same movement is done in 2nd and 5th positions.

If temps levé is done from 5th position to 5th position moving forward, backward or sideways with a small spring, this *pas* is called sus-sous. At the instant of the rise onto pointes, the feet must be closed abruptly, one foot behind the other, giving the impression of one foot. When the *pas* is executed in this way, it gives a good polish to the dance (fig. 95).

2) *Échappé on pointe*. Demi-plié in 5th position, push away with the heels, jump into 2nd position on pointe, then lower back into demi-plié in 5th position. You can also finish in 5th position with a change of feet (fig. 96). Échappé in croisé and in effacé are done from 5th and [into] 4th positions.

Fig. 96. Échappé on pointe

3) *Glissade*. Stand in 5th position, right foot front; demi-plié, slide the toes of the right foot along the floor to the side (to step to the right), and rise onto this foot on pointe, taking the left foot quickly into 5th position on pointe (fig. 97). Then lower into demi-plié.

Fig. 97. Glissade (on pointe)

4) *Temps lié*. Stand in 5th position, right foot front, with both arms in 1st position; demi-plié, and slide the toes of the right foot along the floor to the front in croisé, remaining in plié on the left leg. Step up onto pointe on the right foot, taking the left arm from 1st position to 3rd position and the right to the side into 2nd position, and closing the left leg into 5th position back on pointe. Lower into demi-plié in 5th position (en face), bringing the left arm into 1st position; slide the toes of the right foot to the side in 2nd position, opening the left arm to the side and leaving the left leg in plié. Transfer the weight onto the right foot, standing on pointe, and close the left foot into 5th position front on pointe, [then] lower the arms to preparatory position (figures 98 and 99). Repeat with the other foot. The same is done to the back. The head complies with proper épaulement.

one   two   three   four

Fig. 98. Temps lié on pointe (1st part)

four   three   two   one

Fig. 99. Temps lié on pointe (2nd part)

5) *Assemblé soutenu.* Stand in 5th position, right foot front, do a demi-plié, while opening the right leg to the side, the toes sliding along the floor; pull the leg into 5th position back, brightly springing onto pointe on both feet, left foot front. Push well from the heel of the left foot. Lower into demi-plié in 5th position (and do the same movement with the left leg) (fig. 100).

6) *Jeté on pointe.* Stand in 5th position, demi-plié, take the right leg with the toes on the floor to the side, along the floor and up to a height of 45°. Bring the right leg behind the left, and jump onto pointe, at the same time lifting the left foot sur le cou-de-pied, then lower into demi-plié on the right leg, opening the left leg to the side, and continue the movement with the other leg (fig. 101). *Jeté* on pointe is done also to the front and back,

Fig. 100. Assemblé soutenu

Fig. 101. Jeté on pointe

in croisé, effacé and écarté, in the same way. This *pas* introduces the poses and movements on pointe on one foot. In more senior classes, the poses are practiced at 90°; having slightly opened preliminarily to a small développé in the desired direction, rise onto pointe in arabesque, attitude or other poses.

7) *Sissonne simple.* We begin to study this at the barre. Stand in 5th position, right foot front, demi-plié, jump onto the left foot on pointe, raising the right foot sur le cou-de-pied front, and finish in 5th position demi-plié (fig. 102). It is also possible to do the reverse: jump onto the right foot on pointe, raising the left foot sur le cou-de-pied back, and finish in 5th position (fig. 103); or change legs, i.e., placing the foot that is raised behind or, vice versa, in front.

Later, sissonne simple is practiced in the centre, with the leg raised higher – to the knee.

Fig. 102. Sissonne simple

Fig. 103. Sissonne simple

8) *Sissonne ouverte*. This movement is done on pointe from 5th position in all the poses, beginning gradually from the least difficult [form].

Demi-plié, jump onto pointe on one foot, opening the other leg with a low développé at 45° to the front, or to 2nd position (fig. 104) or back; finish by lowering into demi-plié in 5th position. Later, this is done as a big sissonne (grande sissonne) – the leg opening to 90° in the same way, in all directions and poses.

Fig. 104. Sissonne ouverte at 45° in 2nd position

Sissonne can be done in different directions; for example, from 5th position to 1st arabesque: after the demi-plié, jumping onto pointe to the side and striking the pose; finish by lowering into demi-plié in 5th position (fig. 105). All these sissonnes may be done an unlimited number of times [consecutively] without

Fig. 105. Sissonne to 1st arabesque

changing the pose; lower each time into demi-plié (making sure that the arabesque leg maintains the proper height), and repeat the movement.

All the movements on pointe: 1) must always be connected by a plié, and 2) should rise to pointe with a small jump.

As for the execution of jumps on pointe, these should be done with the foot well-supported and the arch and ankle taut, eliminating all softness. These jumps on pointe belong to one of the most difficult areas of pointe-work, and their development requires serious attention.

Often, the concentrated stress in the ankle is passed on to the rest of the body, and it also becomes tense, which makes the dancer look quite inartistic. Despite the back being held erect (as described when I discussed aplomb), the arms and head should remain free. Only then will these jumps on pointe have the appearance of ease, without which the dance artistry is lost.

X. TOURS

Tour is an old French term common in choreographic literature as a designation for the turning of the body on one foot. The term *pirouette*, as regards the practice of the female dancer, must be considered to have died out, and [today] we speak only of "tours". Male dancers have still kept the term, and they use it mainly for a sequence of multiple turns in place on one leg – for example, their "big pirouette" (grande pirouette) in 2nd position at 90°.

So, here, we shall only use the term "tours".

PREPARATION FOR STUDIES

In approaching the study of tours in their most elementary form on demi-pointe, I recommend following the same progressive approach and attentiveness as in the subsequent study of turns on pointe. The elementary exercises cannot be neglected, as they accustom the legs to the correct position in all stages of the turn. Without the gradual study of all the leg movements that go into the execution of turns, the student can easily acquire a negligent, approximate manner of execution. Just as strict is the preparation of how the arms participate in the execution of turns. Subsequent correction of a wrongly-learned execution of turns will demand incomparably more time and energy than learning it correctly from the start. Therefore, I recommend the following approach for studying tours – at first on a demi-pointe, then on full-pointe.

Teaching children to turn the body is the first and most preparatory stage in the elementary grades. The following types of turns are inserted into the exercises at the barre:

1) turns on two feet;
and in later classes:

2) turns on one foot; (in any exercise in which it is necessary to change feet, they are switched quickly at the outset of the turn, and the [turning] movement proceeds on the other foot);

3) turns on the standing leg, with a return to the starting position.

This last type of turn is studied in the [more] senior classes and is applied to: battements tendus, petits battements sur le cou-de-pied and battements développé, etc. All these movements are accompanied by a change of the hands at the barre.

All this, however, only accustoms the body to turning in general. We really approach the study of turns in the sequence that follows.

It is necessary to begin with turns on two feet and then continue to turns on one foot, in the following order: 1) tours with dégagé[1], 2) from 4th position, and finally, 3) from 5th position, then on to turns in attitude, in arabesque, in 2nd position, etc. After having studied these on demi-pointe, we then study them on pointe, following the same sequence of preparatory exercises. Tours on pointe in attitude, arabesque and 2nd position are learned at the conclusion of one's choreographic education.

Let's begin with the simplest turns *in the centre* – the *turns on two feet.* This movement is a type of battement soutenu.

En dehors. From 5th position, right foot front, do a demi-plié, and simultaneously open the right leg to 2nd position, with the toes extended to the floor; rise onto demi-pointe, simultaneously closing the right leg tightly into 5th position back, turn to the right, forcing the rotation en dehors, and finish the movement by returning the right leg to the front again in 5th position. In this movement, the arms play an important role in helping the legs. When beginning the movement, open them into 2nd position at half-height, then, during the turn, they come together below, with an elastic movement into preparatory position.

En dedans. From the same position, after the demi-plié, take the left foot away to the side, and draw it to the front in 5th position, simultaneously rising to demi-pointe, with the legs

---

[1] This antiquated term is no longer applicable. I use it in the traditional sense for this type of turn.

stretched. Then turn to the right (en dedans), and finish with the right foot front, using the same movement of the arms. Be careful that, in both movements, en dehors and en dedans, the leg does not describe an unnecessary arc on the floor, but rather returns in a straight line from the 2nd to the 5th position.

The following exercise is a *transition from one foot to the other*, with a half-turn on demi-pointe.

4   En dehors   3   2   En dedans   1

Fig. 106. Transition from one foot to another with half-turns

From 5th position, right foot front, do a demi-plié, dégagé to 2nd position with the right leg, the toes extended to the floor, then rise onto this foot on demi-pointe, and take the left behind into 5th position, with a half-turn en dedans. Stop facing back, do a demi-plié, dégagé the left leg to 2nd position, and rise to demi-pointe on the left foot, while closing the right front into 5th position with a half-turn en dehors (fig. 106).

The arms open to 2nd position with the dégagé, and during the turn, they come together in preparatory position with the same elastic movement as in the previous exercise.

A similar movement is the *Jeté on demi-pointe* with a half-turn: with each change to the other foot, there is a move to the side, turning a half-turn and alternating en face – back – en face – back, and so on. The leg moves to the side, lifting each time to 45° (fig. 107). In the dégagé to 2nd position with the right leg, the right arm is in 1st position and the left in 2nd; in the dégagé with the left leg, the left arm is in 1st position and the right in 2nd.

This movement accustoms us to maintaining control of the body, especially in the second part of the turn, when the body

4
two

3
one

2
two

1
one

Fig. 107. Jeté on demi-pointe with a half-turn

turns away from the audience. Attention must be paid to the turn-out of the knee over the foot during the plié.

Having studied the execution of the turns on demi-pointe mentioned above, the student may easily begin with their execution on pointe.

After these preparatory exercises, you can begin to do tours in their simplest form.

TOURS WITH PRÉPARATION DÉGAGÉE

En dehors. Stand in 5th position, right foot front, demi-plié and dégagé the left leg to 45° in 2nd position; bring the left leg in front of the right on demi-pointe, and turn on the left foot, having lifted the right foot sur le cou-de-pied front. Fall into demi-plié on the right leg, the left being extended to the side at 45°, and continue.

These tours can be done on the diagonal, in which case, when falling onto the right leg, the left leg must be opened to the side in diagonal.

The arms move in the following way: during the dégagé, open them into 2nd position at half-height, and during the turn, close them into preparatory position. The force necessary for the turn is drawn from this movement of the arms. During the turns, the arms should not be pulled in sharply, as this will throw you off-balance (fig. 108).

Fig. 108. Tour with dégagé, en dehors

En dedans. The following is the form most often used: from 5th position, right foot front, demi-plié and dégagé with the right leg to 2nd position at 45°; on this same foot, without bringing it in to the left foot, do a tour en dedans on demi-pointe, with the left foot sur le cou-de-pied front; fall onto the left leg in demi-plié, with the right foot sur le cou-de-pied front, and from here, continue (fig. 109). Later, these turns are done on the diagonal, and then in a circle, with the left foot sur le cou-de-pied back during the turn. The body turns to effacé at the beginning of the movement, and the foot is held sur le cou-de-pied back during the tour.

Fig. 109. Tour with dégagé, en dedans

The arms do the same movements as in the tours en dehors.

The next study is of tours from 4th position, which, due to their preparation in 4th position, are easier than those that follow – the tours from 5th position.

TOURS FROM 4ᵀᴴ POSITION

The preparatory exercises, in which all of the movements in these tours are practiced without turns, should be done in the elementary grades.

En dehors. Stand in 4th position croisée, left foot front; demiplié (fig. 110, *1*), and push off from the floor with *both* heels. It is absolutely essential to rise onto a *high* demi-pointe[2] on the left leg as if jumping up on it with a short push-off (this is the method of the Italian School, which should be adhered to strictly, as it is of great help in the execution of tours), with the right foot placed tightly sur le cou-de-pied front, just as cleanly as it would be held in correct execution of the turn. Maintain this pose, try to find a firm balance, and finish in 4th position demiplié, right foot back.

The arms: in the first pose, the right arm is extended to the front, as in 3rd arabesque (the body, too, is in 3rd arabesque position), and the left arm is open to the side, with both hands slightly raised. In the rise onto demi-pointe, the arms join together

Fig. 110. Tours en dehors from 4ᵗʰ position

[2] When doing the exercises on demi-pointe, in order not to lose the turn-out that is so essential in a classical exercise, it is not necessary to lift the heel as far as indicated in fig. 112. Only for a strong movement – such as, for example, tours with a sharp release of the heel from the floor – does the foot rise onto a high demi-pointe, because, if turns on low demi-pointe are stable, the turn-out will not be lost with the [greater] efforts of rising to high demi-pointe.

in a 1ˢᵗ position at 45° (it is important to observe that they are well-rounded and strong in early studies), and in the final pose, open only the hands, leaving the arms in the same position.

We prepare for tours en dehors with this exercise, as it contains both the preparation and the finish of the turn.

En dedans. Tours en dedans are studied in the same manner. The difference is in how the force is taken. In tours en dehors, from the 4ᵗʰ position, both feet are pushed away from the floor. In tours en dedans, however, the push is from the left heel only; open the right leg to 2ⁿᵈ position at 45°, and jump sharply onto demi-pointe on the left foot, pulling the right foot in tightly sur le cou-de-pied. At the start in 4ᵗʰ position, the left arm is rounded in front in 1ˢᵗ position, and the right is open in 2ⁿᵈ; with the dégagé, both arms are open in 2ⁿᵈ position, and when the right foot attaches sur le cou-de-pied, they join together in 1ˢᵗ position at 45° and then in the final pose in 4ᵗʰ position demi-plié (with the right foot back), the arms stay in preparatory position, the hands just opening slightly (fig. 111).

Fig. 111. Tour en dedans from 4ᵗʰ position

It should be noted that we also can finish the tour with the right foot front in 5ᵗʰ position. Once the students are sufficiently prepared, they are taught to do one turn, and later, two and three. Then both the preparatory exercises and the actual turns are practiced on pointe.

When beginning the study of turns, we should not lose sight [of the fact] that the force for the turn is taken from the arms,

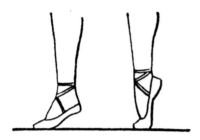

Fig. 112. Low and high demi-pointe.

and never from the [upper] body, which should be still. We should also remember that the force is not taken from the shoulders and that the turn is executed only around one's own axis.

TOURS FROM 5TH POSITION

Tours from 5th position are more complicated: without having a preparatory movement as in 4th position, which gives a convenient push, we must rely here mainly on work of the arms. The preparatory exercises are similar to those of the preceding [turns].

En dehors. Stand in 5th position, right foot front; demi-plié, jump up to demi-pointe on the left foot with the same push off from the floor as in the preceding exercise, lifting the right foot sur le cou-de-pied front.

The right arm is in 1st position, and the left is open in 2nd; in the turn, the arms, coming together in 1st position at 45°, give the turning force at the moment of the spring up to demi-pointe, as in the first example. One can finish the exercise in 5th position, right foot back, or in 4th position.

1   2   3   4   5

Fig. 113. Tour en dehors from 5th position

All this is then done with a tour. Note that, when doing several turns consecutively, the right foot closes into 5th position front, not back, at the end of each turn (fig. 113).

En dedans. For a tour en dedans, stand in 5th position, right foot front; demi-plié, and spring onto the right foot, with the left foot sur le cou-de-pied front. Lower into 5th position with the left foot front. When finishing the exercise in 5th position, it is necessary to contain the movement strongly, in order to achieve precise execution; finishing in 4th position is easier and does not require such precise restraint (fig. 114).

Despite the fact that the left foot rises, the arms do the same movements as for tours en dehors[3].

Fig. 114. Tour en dedans from 5th position

TOURS IN ATTITUDE, IN ARABESQUE AND OTHER POSES

We prepare for the study of these big turns with exercises on demi-pointe, similar to the preparation for small turns, with the same preparatory poses.

En dehors. We begin with the preparation for tours in attitude. The preparatory pose is 4th position, right foot back; the right arm is stretched to the front, the left is in 2nd position. Plié,

---

[3] In preparing the study of arm placement in tours, they are in 1st position; but in the final execution (especially when doing two or more tours, and yet more so with a partner), the arms need to be held slightly lower; see figures 110, 111, 113 and 114.

then rise onto demi-pointe on the left leg, as described above, assuming the pose attitude croisée, and finish by lowering the heel.

When doing a tour on demi-pointe, if this tour is used in an adagio, it is preferable to finish it on demi-pointe without changing the pose. As in the previous exercises, one must push away from the plié in 4th position with both heels, and at the beginning of the tour, push to rise onto demi-pointe on the left foot, fixing the pose in that same instant, and then turn, all without losing the turn-out of the left leg.

It is difficult to gather force here, especially for two or three turns, so greater dexterity must be developed: in the push of the heel and the upward throw of the hands, which are opened during the preparation, with the palms turned downward. At the same instant of rising for the tour, the arms are gathered into the required pose. All this also serves as force.

Tours in 3rd and 4th arabesques and à la seconde are studied from the same preparation (the right hand, thrown at the beginning of the tour in the direction of a tours en dehors, helps to gain force); and the same technique can be used for tours in développé effacé front, i.e., for tours in which the right leg rises to the front during a turn to the right.

En dedans. The force for tours en dedans is taken differently, as we learned in the preparatory exercises. Take a preparation in 4th position, right foot back, with the left arm in 1st position and the right arm open to the side; rise to demi-pointe in attitude effacée, then, as in the preceding exercise, lower the heel. When we begin to do this as a tour, force is taken from the left arm, which is thrown open to 2nd position, while the right arm is raised in attitude, and the entire weight of the body is shifted onto the supporting leg (p. 102).

The preparation for tours in 1st or 2nd arabesque is executed in the same way, although in these cases, the left arm opens to the 1st or 2nd arabesque pose. This arm must be solid, and precisely in the right direction, otherwise it can easily shake or pull the body forward (see description of arabesques on p. 103). For turns with the leg front in développé croisé, the force is taken as for à la seconde, but, during the turn, the leg comes to the front in croisé, and the left arm passes first through 2nd position, while, in doing a tour à la seconde, it is necessary that the leg (together with the arm) line up in 2nd position.

TOURS À LA SECONDE AT 90° (FROM 2ND POSITION)

For tours à la seconde from 2nd position, I prefer the Italian method to the French, because it is more accurate and dynamic and, thus, more modern.

We study it with the following preparatory exercise.

En dehors. Stand in 5th position, right foot front; demi-plié, rise onto demi-pointe in 5th, with the arms front in 1st position; they then open to 2nd position, and the right leg is simultaneously thrown with a grand battement to 2nd position at 90°, then lower to the floor on both legs in 2nd position demi-plié, the right arm closing into 1st position, and with a short, sharp throw, the right leg is raised to 2nd position, while rising onto demi-pointe on the left, and the arms are thrown open to 2nd position. Stay on the left leg, on demi-pointe, with the right leg à la seconde at 90° (fig. 115).

Tour à la seconde is [also] studied with a plié in 2nd position, and one must be careful that the heel of the left [supporting] foot does not turn in at the beginning of the turn, but rather maintains its turn-out as long as possible, which is crucial in achieving a good tour à la seconde.

After the preparation in 2nd position, force for the turn is taken by throwing out [lit.: discarding] the right arm to 2nd position, and the shoulders must remain even; the right shoulder should not be taken forward, thinking that this will help gain force.

En dedans. The preparation for this tour en dedans uses the same plié in 2nd position, then the left leg is raised, and the turn goes en dedans.

During the preparation, the right arm is in 1st position, and the left is open in 2nd; the force is taken from the right arm and, I repeat, never from the shoulder.

The French method differs in that, from the 5th position, the right leg does a short développé à la seconde, then plié in 2nd position, and so on.

Fig. 115. Tour à la seconde at 90° from 2nd position

There are also tours sur le cou-de-pied from 2nd position, and they are similar to those described above, with the difference being that the leg is thrown not to 90°, but to 45°, and during the tour, the [right] foot closes to the left leg sur le cou-de-pied. During the execution of this turn, the arms come together in preparatory position (fig. 116).

Fig. 116. Préparation for tour sur le cou-de-pied from 2nd position

TOURS FROM 5TH POSITION (FROM A DEEP PLIÉ)

The method for executing adagio turns from grand plié in 5th position is completely different: when beginning the plié, keep the heels on the floor as long as possible; however, having reached the deepest point (i.e., when the heels start to pull away from the floor), extend the leg on which the turn is to be executed, and immediately rise high onto demi-pointe, keeping the back absolutely straight, and without the slightest wobble. The arms, opening into 2nd position at the beginning of the plié, go smoothly downward to preparatory position, and at the instant of the rise, they take the same form as in the execution of turns from 4th and 5th positions.

TOURS CHAÎNES

Tours chaînés, déboulés – that is the Parisian terminology. I use both names, because they are very expressive, and, in different ways, they both characterize the movement. A suddenly racing chain of little circles – here is a definition arising from the name, and it gives an accurate picture of the *pas*. Chaînés are done at a very fast pace, each turn in 1/8 or 1/16 [a half- or quarter-beat]. The movement travels on the diagonal (from point *6* to point *2* on our diagram, fig. 2b). This *pas* often ends a variation, but is [also] used to great effect in the composition of variations or other dances. Chaînés are executed as follows.

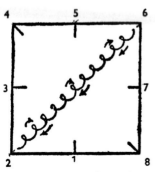

Fig. 117. Direction of tours chaînés

If the movement is done to the right, the turn starts on the right foot, which steps forward onto the diagonal; finishing the turn, one must put the left foot forward [in relation] to the place where the right was (never backward). The impulse begins by throwing the right arm forward; then the two hands connect in front of the body. In early studies, the arm movement is repeated with each turn. Once the technique is fully assimilated, and the turning rate increases, the dancer no longer has time to throw the arms open and helps instead with small movements of the arms in the same direction, but not so big as to delay or slow down the movement. At a fast pace, having given a push with the leg the first time to the right, move in the same direction by [the force of] inertia, although the feet do not take a [real] step, but remain close to one another. The whole movement is helped by the arms (see above). To do chaînés well, one must possess great agility, and the back must be held strongly and absolutely straight, not bending in any direction. The movement develops into a rapid chain of turns, which comes to an end with an unexpected stop, staying in whatever final pose, as if frozen.

Virtuosity in this movement has reached a high degree, and the turning rates attained are dizzying. Chaînés are done high on demi-pointe and also on pointe.

It must be added that tours chaînés, jeté par terre and some other steps in dance are often executed in a circle around the stage.

TOURS EN L'AIR

These tours are the domain of men's dancing, which I will not touch on here. Although both the steps and the daily lessons are identical, for men's dancing, it is necessary to adapt these to more difficult movements, due to the male dancer's stronger muscles. Men also have a big advantage in their work: no dancing on pointe, the study of which consumes such great effort and time – and this saves the male dancer's strength and gives him time to refine those *pas* that are in common with female dancers, but which take on a different character and degree of virtuosity in the male versions. In men's dancing, less time is given over to the adagio. On the one hand, adagio is necessary for women, as a way of strengthening the body, which is by nature more flexible and weaker than the male body, and on the other hand, this very flexibility allows a woman to achieve those absolutely perfect lines, which, with very rare exceptions, remain inaccessible to male dancers.

If I touch here on turns in the air, it is partly because both men and women can do these tours; and contemporary choreographers often have women do them.

Stand in 5th position, right foot front, deep demi-plié (almost, but not quite tearing the heels away from the floor), with the left arm open to the side and the right in front in 1st position. Push away with the heels, and, having risen into the air, take a tour in the air, the arms joining together during the tours. Land in 5th position, demi-plié, right foot back, with the arms slightly open in front and the body erect. Be careful that the right shoulder does not go forward before the jump to help gain momentum, i.e., to keep the body absolutely en face.

GENERAL COMMENTS ABOUT TOURS

The first prerequisite for a good turn is an absolutely straight and held body. One must not lose [sight of] the spot where one stops, always feeling where en face is, in order not to become dizzy. In the popular 32 fouettés, for example, if the performer loses the spot in front of her and is not facing perfectly front in the plié each time, all will be lost.

Theoretically speaking, during tours and in all types of turns, you need to leave the head facing the audience as long as possible. But the approach to this work of the head in tours must be very careful. One must be careful not to incline the head sideways or off the axis around which the turn is executed. Ignoring this will easily knock you off balance. To achieve the multiple turns that are required in today's technique, one must moderate the actions of the head, emphasizing only the focus, i.e., in every passage en face, look at the audience, and maintain this focus as long as possible.

In turns with the support of a gentleman, the man must, first of all, be standing solidly. Inexperienced partners lean backward involuntarily at the beginning of a turn and then lean forward at the last turn, inevitably pushing their partners and knocking them off balance. He should stand as if rooted to the spot, while his partner turns between the palms of his hands. The rest depends on her. If she can turn well, she should not be assisted in the turn; if she is a weak turner, then the partner needs to help her to turn with his hands.

In partnered adagio, there are various kinds of pirouettes. Tours can be done from a preparation in 5th position on pointe, with the force taken as follows: standing on pointe on the left foot, take the right leg to croisé front, throw it forcefully to the side, avoiding any change of position of the hips (to take force from the leg), and then bend the knee, the right foot going toward the left knee, back or front, to turn. The partner helps by holding her at the waist, at first pushing her right side slightly forward, and then, with the swing, pushing her into the turn with his left hand.

From the same preparation, the dancer can do tours holding on to the middle finger of her partner's right hand, which is held above her head. The dancer should hold on to his middle finger with her entire right hand, and the partner assists her a bit by circling his finger. But the force is taken from the same strong swing of the leg, and the deftness of the turn is concentrated in the skillful help of the partner's finger.

In any partnered turn, the arms must be held tightly closed in front of the body, one over another. And yet one final note: in a preparation for tours en dehors with one arm front, the turn must be taken from there, without swinging the arm before the turn.

Here, we have wandered from the subject of this book, since it is not our task to write about partnering.

XI. OTHER KINDS OF TURNS

ADAGIO TURNS

In adagio *in the centre*, slow turns are done on the entire [i.e., flat] foot, and these are sometimes used in choreography. They can be done in all the poses: attitude, arabesque, 2nd position at 90° and développé front. These slow turns are made with small shifts of the heel in the required direction.

RENVERSÉ

Renversé, as the name indicates, is a backward tipping of the body during a turn. It has various forms and is one of the most complicated movements in the education of a classical dancer. Renversé is extremely difficult to describe, and nothing here can replace live demonstration and instruction in the classroom from a teacher who can dance it masterfully.

Let's describe here the following kinds of renversé.

Renversé en dehors. This movement begins with an attitude croisée; demi-plié, incline the body slightly forward, accentuating the movement by inclining the head, then jump up to demi-pointe in a pose attitude, at the same time concentrating all the impetus of movement in the back. The back is first straightened, then curved strongly to the back as soon as the turn en dehors begins; [the turn is] done by the *body*, and the legs follow this movement only at the last moment, doing a pas de bourrée en dehors when the body, having changed its center of gravity through the forces of the turn, makes the legs take a step. It is the force used for the transfer of weight that makes the legs move, instead of the leg turning the body. For the effectiveness of this *pas*, in 3/4 time: on *one*, the body must incline and begin the turn, rising onto demi-pointe on the left foot in attitude; on

Fig. 118. Renversé en dehors

two, on the right leg, with the back facing the audience, the body is held, and the back is strongly curved, and the head is inclined in profile position. This pose is held as long as possible (the entire *second beat* [lit.: quarter]), so that only a minimal part of the measure remains for the final turn of the body and the step (pas de bourrée) (fig. 118).

The common mistake of dancers without sufficiently virtuosic technique is to turn the body in the renversé by the movement of the arms and steps of the feet, forcing the body to follow the [directional] inertia of the arms. Without mentioning that only the *name* of this pas will remain, with such an execution, the dancer will lose control: as soon as she has to repeat the *pas* several times in succession, she will be carried sideways; and searching for her balance, she will then lose the rhythm, etc.

Renversé en dedans is the reverse movement, and it is much easier and simpler to execute. Done from a développé en avant croisé, the body bends forward and then does the same backward bend, with a delay in the pose croisée, as in the en-dehors, and with the steps going in the opposite direction, en dedans.

Renversé en écarté is done from 4th arabesque. From this 4th arabesque, the right leg bends at the beginning of the turn, the toe of the right foot touching the knee of the supporting leg en tire-bouchon, on demi-pointe[1]. At the same time, the body

---

[12] En tire bouchon – a position with the leg raised to 90° and bent at the knee, with the toes pointed and touching the knee of the supporting leg. When a pirouette is done in this pose, the impression is of a cork-screw turning.

inclines strongly forward to the right [and] toward the knee of the supporting leg. The body turns en dedans, bending to the back, and at the same moment, the heel is placed quickly and firmly on the floor; together with the [movement of the] body, the other leg opens to écarté back, stopping there firmly, while the heel of the supporting leg is lowered.

The arms, from the 4th arabesque, meet with a strong movement into preparatory position while the leg is en tire-bouchon, and, simultaneously to the sharp opening of the leg and body, they rise into 3rd position in écarté back. This movement, just as the first form of renversé, requires a strongly-developed body and the dancer's ability to take a movement with the back.

FOUETTÉ EN TOURNANT À 45°

En dehors. Done from demi-plié on the left leg, this time the right leg opens to 2nd position at 45°; tour en dehors on the left leg, and during the tour, raise the right foot behind the calf, then quickly bring it around to the front of the calf. Stop again in demi-plié, opening the arms and leg to 2nd position. During the movement of the leg into 2nd position, the arms also open to 2nd position, and they are closed into preparatory position during the tour.

En dedans. Done in the same way, but the foot is taken first in front of the calf, and then behind it.

When fouettés are done many times in succession, one must take something like a "swing". You can start like this: do a pas de bourrée en dedans, and then begin the fouettés. But this is not very reliable, as it concentrates the body's balance poorly and can knock one off one's center. It all depends on the individual's body.

A more reliable way [lit.: trick] is to take a préparation in 4th position, jump onto pointe, doing one tour en dehors, and continue to turn, doing the fouettés.

This *pas*, which, not so long ago, seemed to be the limit of difficulty and virtuosity, is now done easily by dancers of the corps de ballet.

GRAND FOUETTÉ

Although this kind of fouetté is done without a turn, I describe it here with the others of the same name.

The grand fouetté that we have developed is rather unique. It has something from both the French and Italian Schools. First, we will analyze the Italian fouetté, in which the body remains en face all the time.

En debors. Pose croisée, left leg back. Coupé on the left leg on demi-pointe, opening the arms to 2nd position during the coupé, and lower into demi-plié on the left leg, taking the left arm to 1st position and leading the right leg, half-bent, to the front at 90°; rise onto demi-pointe on the left leg, quickly leading the right leg around in a grand rond de jambe to the back, and finish in demi-plié on the left leg in 3rd arabesque en face. During the grand rond de jambe, the arms do the following port de bras: the left arm rises through 3rd position into 2nd, while the right goes to 3rd position and passes through 1st position into 3rd arabesque as the left leg goes into plié.

I will now describe that fouetté which my girls do, although it is nearly impossible to explain and make comprehensible through words the "method" that the movement employs and how the coordination between the arm and leg movements is achieved. This fouetté is controlled by the arms, which inform the movement of the entire body. This must be very well understood and the form mastered, in order to be able to do it onstage without fear of losing one's balance.

Préparation, do the same coupé, opening the arms to 2nd position, and take the left arm to 1st position while on demi-pointe, then demi-plié on the left leg, turning the body to effacé. Taking the right leg, half-bent, to effacé front at 45° and, bending the body toward the leg, pull in the right side of the body and arch the left side; rise onto demi-pointe, taking the leg through a grand rond de jambe, and during its passage, turn the body to attitude effacée at 90° and above, as with this swing, the leg can be raised to maximum height; simultaneously, the left arm rises to 3rd position and opens into 2nd position, while the right arm goes up from 2nd position to 3rd position and a pose effacée. Lower into demi-plié.

Fig. 119. Grand fouetté

Done in this way, the movement takes on a more plastic, classical form, whereas the Italian fouetté is a bit dry and schematic, without the softening transitional croisée and effacée poses, etc.

En dedans – the right leg is bent to the back in effacé at 45°, and the body bends toward the leg; the right arm is in 1st position, the left is open in 2nd. Rise to demi-pointe on the left leg, doing a grand rond de jambe in the same way as specified for the en-dehors, lifting the right leg to the front at 90° and higher, in effacé.

The right arm, after passing through preparatory position, opens to 2nd position, and the left arm goes up to 3rd position. Finish in demi-plié on the left leg. These movements can also be done with a jump, observing the same rules.

GRAND FOUETTÉ EN TOURNANT

En dedans. This type is more common than the en-dehors that follows. Take a pose croisée front, left foot front, and lower into demi-plié on the left leg, then jump up to demi-pointe on it, and throw the right leg out to 2nd position at 90° with a grand battement jeté. Throw the arms up to 2nd position. Lower on the left leg in demi-plié, turning, to brush the floor with the right foot close to the supporting foot, throwing it to the front with a grand battement at 90° in the direction of point 6 (see fig. 2b), pivoting, while rising onto demi-pointe and bending the body to the back, and complete the turn en dedans, keeping the right foot at the same height to end the movement in 3rd arabesque in demi-plié (this may also finish in 1st arabesque).

As the leg moves forward, the arms pass through preparatory position, upward through 3rd position, and finish in arabesque (fig. 120).

Fig. 120. Grand fouetté en tournant

En dehors. Croisée pose, left leg back, coupé, demi-plié on the left leg, throw the right leg out to 2nd position at 90°, rising onto demi-pointe on the left leg, open the arms to 2nd position, throw the right leg through 1st position on the floor into 3rd arabesque in demi-plié, taking the arms through preparatory position and also into 3rd arabesque, and turn en dehors on demi-pointe to croisé front at 90°, [finishing] in demi-plié and placing the arms in the required pose[2].

---

[2] While fouetté at 45° is executed in one count, i.e., *one beat*, all forms of grand fouetté are done in two counts, i.e., *two beats*. Each *beat* falls on the plié. The same [applies] for the grand fouetté sauté, which is [also] executed in *two beats*.

Grand fouetté en tournant is also done from 2nd position, and at first, it resembles the fouetté at 45°; but it is done in two movements. It begins on the *upbeat*, throwing the leg out with a short movement to 2nd position at 90° on demi-pointe, with the arms also opening out to 2nd position; on the *first beat* [lit.: *first quarter*] – plié on the supporting leg, then take the turn, passing the foot from behind the knee to in front of it, ending on the *second beat* in plié, with the foot in front of the knee (at the same time, the arms meet in preparatory position).

Like the fouetté at 45°, this *pas* is done only on pointe, without a jump, and is specific to female technique.

GRAND FOUETTÉ EN TOURNANT SAUTÉ

The same *pas* can also be done as a jump. Begin the same way, and after the demi-plié on the left leg, throw the right leg out to 2nd position; the left foot detaches from the floor with a jump, while the right leg is thrust out in the way previously described, and the turn is also done in the air, during the jump off the left leg.

1ST EXAMPLE OF LESSON*

The following is an example for the senior classes, to be done on demi-pointe.[1]

EXERCISES AT THE BARRE

1) *Pliés in the five positions* (in two measures *of 4/4*):
one slow, *in four beats* [lit.: *four quarters*], another quickly, *in two beats*, and *in two beats*, rise onto demi-pointe.
2) *Battements tendus.*
To the front: *in one beat each*; two with plié, two without plié; three in one half-beat each (a pause on the 4th half-beat); seven in one quarter-beat each (pause – on the 8th quarter-beat).
To the side: the same.
Back: the same.
Again to the side: the same.
Repeat it all.
On the other leg.[2]
3) *Battements fondus* and *frappés* (combined) (*eight measures of 4/4*).
Front: one slow fondu *in two beats* and two quick, *in one beat each*.
To the side: the same.
Back: the same.
Again to the side: the same.
Two slow frappés *in one beat each*, three quick *in half-beats* (pause *on the 4th half-beat*) – [repeat] four times.
Repeat the entire combination, beginning from the back.
On the other leg.

---

[1] In the form used in the program of the classical ballet curriculum and the program of introductory tests at the Leningrad State Choreographic School.

[2] Each movement of an exercise is *always* executed on one leg, then the other.

* The graphic layout is that of the original 1948 edition. *Ed.*

4) *Ronds de jambe* (*two measures of 4/4*).

Three fast ronds de jambe par terre en dehors *in three half-beats*; *on the 4th half-beat*, rise to demi-pointe, having opened the leg to 2nd position. Three ronds de jambe en l'air en dehors *in three half-beats* (*on the 4th half-beat* – a pause), four ronds de jambe en l'air en dehors *in four half-beats*. Plié sur le cou-de-pied and tour en dehors, *in four half-beats*.

Repeat this entire combination en dedans.

On the other leg.

5) *Battements battus* and *petits battements* (*eight measures of 4/4*).

Four times *in 4 beats*, a double battement battu with a pause in a pose effacée front in plié after each beat. In the following measure, consecutive battements battus with a pause *on the 4th beat* in effacé front in plié.

Four times *in 4 beats*, a petit battement with a pause in 2nd position after each beat. In one measure, consecutive petits battements with a pause in 2nd position and in plié *on the fourth beat*.

Four times *in 4 beats*, a petit battement with a pause in a pose effacée back in plié after each beat. In the following measure, consecutive petits battements with a pause *on the 4th beat* in a pose effacée back in plié.

Repeat the two previously-described measures of petits battements with a pause in 2nd position.

On the other leg.

6) *Développé* (in *two measures of 4/4*).

Extend the right leg to the front with the toes to the floor, doing a demi-plié on the left leg (*1st beat*); raise the right leg to 90°, extending the left knee (*2nd beat*); a small, short balancé with the raised leg (*3rd beat*); take the leg to 2nd position (*4th beat*). Bend the right knee (*1st beat*), open to 2nd arabesque, rising to demi-pointe (*2nd beat*), fall onto the right foot back into demi-plié, the toes of the [left] foot extending forward (*3rd beat*), and quickly rise onto demi-pointe on this foot, lifting the right leg to attitude croisée (*4th beat*), i.e., execute a battement développé tombé.

Do the entire combination in reverse, beginning back.

Third figure – in 2nd position, with all poses to the side: in the first case, the finish is écartée back, in the second, écartée front.

On the other side.

7) *Grands battements jetés balancés* (in *one* measure *of 4/4*).

We begin by taking the left leg to the back and pointing the foot.

Brush the foot through 1st position, throw the leg to the front, then the same way to the back (*1st and 2nd beats*), and twice through 1st position, on into 2nd position (*3rd and 4th beats*).

The next time, having begun front, throw the leg first to the back, then to the front and on into 2nd position.

On the other leg.

It is necessary to counterbalance with the upper body, as is specified for battement balancé.

I believe that this exercise provides full development to the muscles and ligaments. I also think that artificial, unnatural ways of stretching – sometimes practiced with the barre, and sometimes without – are all unnecessary: for example, stretches with the leg on the barre. I seldom recommend such exercises, although the method described below can be of some use.

Stand facing the barre in 1st position, holding it with both hands, with the legs fully stretched. Lean the body to the right, without lifting the heels from the floor; return to the starting position, and do the same to the left. Repeat this several times.

EXERCISES IN THE CENTRE

Due to the limits of time in the lesson, I recommend getting promptly to the program of exercises *in the centre*, which is as follows:

I.   Small adagio (petit adagio). Plié is combined with various types of développés and battements tendus.

II.   In the second small adagio, introduce combinations with battements fondus and frappés, together with ronds de jambe en l'air.

III. In the big adagio, more difficult movements are added, according to the given character of the adagio.

IV.   To start off the *allegro*, I tend to give only small jumps, i.e., low and simple.

V.   *Allegro* with big *pas*.

VI.   For the first *pas on pointe*, I select those that are done on two legs: échappé in 2nd position, then in 4th position. This precaution is necessary, in order to start working new [as yet unused] muscles during the transition to these new movements, despite the fact that the legs are already warmed up.

VII. Finish the lesson by bringing into re-balance all of the muscles and tendons that have been worked until now, with small changements de pieds, and to end nicely and develop the body's flexibility, a port de bras is done.

SMALL ADAGIO

I.   Deep plié in 5th position, a turn and a half en dehors sur le cou-de-pied, pause in 1st arabesque facing back, and continue to turn in the same direction, bringing the leg to croisé front and looking under the right hand in 3rd position; then brush the leg along the floor to 2nd arabesque, plié, and do two tours en dehors in attitude croisée; renversé en dehors to finish. Two battements tendus back with the left foot, two to the front with the right, doing these in one beat each; three quick battements tendus with the left, pause for one half-beat, and repeat with the right leg. Six battements tendus in 2nd position, doing each in one half-beat, and flic-flac en dehors, stopping in 4th position préparation on the left leg, and one or two tours en dehors sur le cou-de-pied.

II. Big relevé en dehors at 90° in 2nd position, pass the leg along the floor to attitude croisée, coupé on the right leg, four ronds de jambe en l'air en dehors with the left leg, plié and pas de bourrée en dehors.

Do the same en dedans.

BIG ADAGIO

Pose croisée with the left leg back, plié, and coupé onto the left leg, ballonné écarté front, stopping in effacé, the right knee bent, with the foot behind the left knee, extend it in the same direction to effacé back, do two tours en dedans sur le cou-de-pied on this leg, ending with the left leg in écarté back and both arms in 3rd position, then turn slowly and lead the lifted leg to 1st arabesque, turning the body toward point *2* (fig. 2b), while the arms open to 2nd position and pass through preparatory position to come together in front, crossed at the wrist. Coupé on the left foot and pas ciseaux (finishing this on the right leg), turn to effacé, left leg front, chassé in effacé, fall onto the left leg in plié, then change onto the right leg, taking an attitude croisée pose, quickly turn en dehors, lower on the left leg in 4th arabesque, renversé in écarté back, pas de bourrée en dehors, two tours en dehors sur le cou-de-pied from 4th position, pas de bourrée en dehors and entrechat-six de volée to the right.

ALLEGRO

I. A big sissonne front to croisé en tournant en dehors, assemblé front, sissonne-soubresaut in attitude effacée on the right leg, take the left foot along the floor to the front, glissade with the right foot to the side and cabriole fermée with the right leg in effacé.

II. a) Saut de basque and renversé sauté en dehors; repeat. Sissonne tombée front in effacé, cabriole in 1st arabesque, pas de bourrée, cabriole in 4th arabesque, sissonne tombée en tournant (en dehors) in croisé front on the right leg; coupé onto the left leg and jeté fermé fondu on the right leg, to the side in 2nd position.

   b) Four sauts de basque on the diagonal with the arms in 3rd position, four chaînés on the diagonal toward point *2* (fig. 2b), préparation in 4th position croisée and two tours en dehors sur le cou-de-pied; finish in 4th position.

III. Préparation croisée, left leg front; grande cabriole fermée in effacé with the right leg, and turn en dedans in 5th position on pointe. Repeat once more. Sissonne tombée to the back in croisé on the right leg, in effacé on the left leg, then on the right leg en tournant en dehors to the front in croisé, cabriole in 4th arabesque and pas de bourrée.[3]

---

[3] This combination may be done to a waltz tempo.

ON POINTE

I. Préparation croisée, left leg back, coupé on the left foot and, on pointe, grand fouetté en dehors with the right leg; bend the knee, and, taking the right leg quickly to the front in croisé, rise onto pointe twice [with] sissonne to 3rd arabesque on the right leg; coupé on the left foot, fouetté on the left leg en dehors at 45°, pas de bourrée en dehors, préparation in 4th position and two tours sur le cou-de-pied en dedans on the right leg, and finish in 5th position.

II. Pas de chat finishing on a bent right leg, développé front in effacé on the left leg on pointe, and immediately take the leg to effacé back, without coming down from pointe. Pas de bourrée (finish on the right leg, the left foot sur le cou-de-pied), fouetté en dedans to the right and en dehors to the left, and finish in 5th position.

III. Do a single tour en dehors on the left leg four times (starting each time with a degagé with the left leg) on the diagonal from point 6 to point 2 (fig. 2b), two fouettés en dehors and a third double fouetté, all on the left leg. Finish in 4th position, right foot back.

2ND EXAMPLE OF LESSON*
(with musical accompaniment)[1]

EXERCISES AT THE BARRE
FOR SENIOR CLASSES AND
THE CLASSE DE PERFECTION

I. PLIÉ IN THE FIVE POSITIONS

Each plié is executed in *two measures of 4/4*: one is a demi-plié, the other – a grand plié. In performing the demi-plié, the arm remains in 2nd position; in the grand plié, the arm accompanies the action, lowering and rising together with the movement of the legs. The transition from one position to another is done with the foot pointed.

---

[1] All the musical examples, with the exception of the excerpts from ballet works by Tchaikovsky and Glazunov [and Minkus – *Ed.*], are working improvisations by S. S. Brodskaya.

* The graphic layout is that of the original 1948 edition. *Ed.*

I

II. BATTEMENTS TENDUS

24 measures of 2/4

Combined with plié in 2nd position

(The leg and arm are opened to 2nd position before the first measure)

1st measure	– Lower the heel to the floor twice, freely relaxing the foot, and then strongly extend the toes each time to lift the heel, each time in *one beat* [lit.: *one quarter*].
2nd measure	– Deep plié in 2nd position – *in two beats* – with a lowering and raising of the arm.
3rd, 4th measures	– This combination of movements is repeated.
5th, 6th, 7th, 8th measures	– Eight battements tendus – *in one beat each.*
8 measures	– (Repeat from the beginning.)
8 measures	– 32 battements tendus jetés, *in half-beats* [lit.: *eighths*].

(The same is done with the other leg.)

II

Allegro non troppo. M.♩=100

III. RONDS DE JAMBE PAR TERRE
AND GRANDS RONDS DE JAMBE JETÉS
8 measures of 4/4

1st measure – Three ronds de jambe par terre en dehors – *in one half-beat each* – stop front *on the 4th half-beat* with the toes pointed to the floor, then take the leg around in one rond de jambe par terre in demi-plié – *in two beats*.

2nd measure – Four grands ronds de jambe jetés en dehors done *in one beat each*.

3rd measure – Three ronds de jambe par terre, *in one half-beat each* – on the 4th half-beat, stop front with the toes on the floor; five ronds de jambe par terre en dehors in *quarter-beats*, and pause *for three quarter-beats*.

4th measure – Four grands ronds de jambe jetés, *in one beat each*.
Repeat the entire exercise en dedans *in four measures*.[2]
Do the same on the other leg.

IV. BATTEMENTS FONDUS AND FRAPPÉS
16 measures of 2/4

1st measure – Battement fondu front – [straightening] *in three quarter-beats* [lit.: *on the dotted eighth*], petit battement *in one quarter-beat*; battement fondu back the same way and at the same speed.

2nd measure – Repeat from the beginning.

3rd & 4th measures – Three fondus to 2nd position – *in one beat* each; plié on the left leg and two fast tours en dehors (from this position) – also *in one beat*.

5th & 6th measures – Eight battements frappés – *in one half-beat each*.

7th & 8th measures – Eight battements doubles frappés – *in one half-beat each*. The entire combination is repeated *in 8 measures*, starting to the back, with the tours [going] en dedans.

---

[2] In performing ronds de jambe par terre at a quick tempo, we must not forget the basic guidelines presented in this book on p. 81-84.

III

IV

V. RONDS DE JAMBE EN L'AIR

4 measures of 4/4

1st measure – Three ronds de jambe en l'air en dehors – *in a half-beat each* – stopping in plié position with the leg in 2nd position *on the 3rd half-beat* – and rise onto demi-pointe *on the 4th half-beat.*

Three ronds de jambe en l'air – *in one half-beat each* – finishing in demi-plié in 5th position (right leg back); *on the 4th half-beat,* do a full turn en dehors on demi-pointe on both feet.

2nd measure – From demi-plié in 5th position, one tour sur le cou-de-pied en dehors – *in one beat.*

Repeat once again – *on the 2nd beat.*

On the 3rd beat – two tours; and open the leg to the side to 2nd position – *on the 4th beat.*

3rd & 4th measures – Repeat en dedans.

VI. PETITS BATTEMENTS

8 measures of 2/4

1st & 2nd measures – Six petits battements, *in one half-beat each*; on *the 7th* [half-beat], a quick switch onto the other foot, with a turn en dehors, and stop *on the 8th* [half-beat].

3rd & 4th measures – Continue the exercise with the other foot, returning to the initial position.

5th, 6th, 7th & 8th measures – Repeat, with a turn en dedans, *in four measures.*

V

VI

VII. BATTEMENTS DÉVELOPPÉS
8 measures of 4/4

1st measure
> *On the 1st beat* – développé front.
> *On the 2nd beat* – bend the leg, bringing the foot to the knee.
> *On the 1st half-beat* – développé back.
> *On the 2nd half-beat* – demi-plié on the left leg.
> *In one beat* – rise up to demi-pointe.

2nd measure
> *On the 1st beat* – turn on the left leg en dehors on half-pointe, right leg front.
> *On the 2nd beat* – turn back again, on demi-pointe, right leg back.
> *On the 3rd beat* – throw the leg to the floor, and brush through 1st position to the front, ending the movement in plié on the left leg[3].
> *On the 4th beat* – rise up to demi-pointe on the left leg (raising the right arm and looking under the arm).

3rd & 4th measures
Repeat the combination of movements from the *1st and 2nd measures* in reverse.

At the transition point for each position, bend the leg, bringing the foot to the knee.

5th measure
> *On the 1st beat* – développé to 2nd position.
> *On the 2nd beat* – bend the leg, bringing the foot to the knee.
> *In one half-beat* – open the right leg to 2nd position.
> *On the 2nd half-beat* – demi-plié on the left leg.
> *In one beat* – rise onto demi-pointe.

6th measure
> *On the 1st beat* – do a quick half-turn en dedans, changing feet, and open the other leg to 2nd position.
> *On the 2nd beat* – do the same thing again, turning back, and open the right leg to 2nd position.
> *On the 3rd beat* – a short downward thrust of the leg, brushing the floor through 1st position and back up to 2nd position (the left leg in plié).
> *On the 4th beat* – rise to demi-pointe and take a pose écartée back.

7th & 8th measures
The entire combination from the 5th measure on is repeated in reverse, i.e., with the turns done *en dehors* and with the final pose écartée front.

---

[3] This movement is executed like a battement jeté balancé, with a backward thrust of the body and, in the second case, with a forward inclination of the body.

VII

VIII. GRANDS BATTEMENTS JETÉS

8 measures of 3/8

Three grands battements jetés – to the front, *in one beat each.*
Three grands battements jetés – to 2nd position.
Three grands battements jetés – to the back.
Three grands battements jetés – to 2nd position.
Repeat the entire combination *in 4 measures.*

In advanced classes, and especially in the Classe de Perfection, this exercise is executed both at the barre and *in the centre* on demi-pointe.

VIII

EXERCISES IN THE CENTRE

I

16 measures of 3/4

From 5th position in demi-plié, développé to the front with the right leg in effacé (*before the first bar*).

4 measures

> *In the 1st measure* – rise to demi-pointe in 1st arabesque.
> *In the 2nd measure* – lower into plié in the same pose.
> *In the 3rd measure* – turn on the left leg en dedans, and finish in effacé front on demi-pointe.
> *In the 4th measure* – plié in this same pose effacée, and continue.
> This step should be done 4 times on the diagonal from point *6* to point *2* of our diagram.

On the other side, the diagonal goes from point *4* to point *8*.

II

The entire *pas* is then executed moving backward from point *2* to point *6*, and from point *8* to point *4* (*also in 16 measures*). From 5th position in demi-plié, développé back in effacé with the left leg (*before the first bar*).

4 measures

> *In the 1st measure* – rise up to demi-pointe on the left foot, opening the right leg to the front in effacé.
> *In the 2nd measure* – lower into plié in the same pose.
> *In the 3rd measure* – a turn on the right leg en dehors, finishing in 2nd arabesque on demi-pointe.
> *In the 4th measure* – plié in this pose.
> Continue, from the beginning (repeat 4 times on each side).

This combination must be performed smoothly and softly, without hopping, and it takes the place of the first adagio *in the centre*.

I

муз. Глазунова *

II

---

* Music: Glazunov

III. BATTEMENTS TENDUS
8 measures of 4/4

1st measure – Four battements tendus to 2nd position – *in one beat each.*

2nd measure – Six battements tendus jetés toward 2nd position [in half-beats]; on the 7th [half-beat], flic-flac en tournant en dedans, and on the 8th, stop in 2nd position.

3rd measure – Four battements tendus to 2nd position – *in one beat each* (the first battement closes in 5th position back).

4th measure – In *one half-beat each*, six battements tendus jetés to the side in 2nd position (starting the first battement in 5th position back), flic-flac en tournant en dehors on the 7th, stop on the 8th with the leg in 2nd position.

5th measure – One tour en dehors with a préparation 2nd position – a slow turn – *in 4 beats*[4].

6th measure – Two tours en dehors with a préparation 2nd position – *in two beats.*

Three tours en dehors with a préparation 2nd position – *in two beats.*

7th measure – One tour en dedans on the right leg with préparation in 2nd position – a slow turn – *in 4 beats.*

8th measure – Two tours en dedans with a préparation 2nd position – *in two beats.*

Three tours en dedans with a préparation 2nd position – *in two beats.*

Repeat with the other leg.

---

[4] The turn executed in *four beats* is, in fact, a slow turn that serves for correct body posture in the study of tours.

III

IV. BATTEMENTS FONDUS AND FRAPPÉS (COMBINED)
8 measures of 2/4

1st & 2nd   – Three battements fondus doubles to the side in 2nd
measures   position – *in one beat each* – and two tours en de-
                hors sur le cou-de-pied – *in one beat.*

3rd measure – Five battements frappés, *in quarter-beats, for three
                half-beats*, and stop in 2nd position.

4th measure – Flic-flac en dehors, finishing in effacé front at 90°
                and holding this pose – *in two beats.*
                (Repeat, starting with the left leg)

1st & 2nd   – Three battements fondus doubles to the side in 2nd
measures   position – *in one beat each* – and two tours en
                dedans sur le cou-de-pied – *in one beat.*

3rd measure – Petits battements – *in quarter-beats, for two beats.*

4th measure – Flic-flac en dedans, finishing in attitude effacée
                and holding this pose – *in two beats.*

IV

V. BIG ADAGIO[5]

4 measures of 4/4

Fifth position in demi-plié, brush the right foot to 2nd position at 45°, and pas de bourrée en tournant en dehors, finishing in 5th position demi-plié, right foot front (these movements are done *before the first bar*).

1st measure – *On the 1st beat* – two tours sur le cou-de-pied en dedans.

On the second beat – stop with the left leg in attitude effacée.

On the third beat – half-turn en dedans to finish back, facing corner 6 (fig. 2b).

On the fourth beat – small thrust of the left leg along the floor through 1st position to croisé front.

2nd measure – Two big chassés croisé back, and stop in this direction toward point 6 on the left leg in 3rd arabesque – *in two beats.*

Quick [half-]turn en dehors to effacé front, two big chassés forward in effacé, stop in 1st arabesque on the right leg – *in two beats.*

3rd measure – Two grands fouettés en dedans with the left leg, finishing in attitude effacée – *in two beats each.*

4th measure – Sissonne tombée croisé back on the left leg – *in one beat.*

Sissonne tombée croisé back on the right leg – *in one beat* (stop in préparation in 4th position).

Three tours en dehors sur le cou-de-pied – *in one beat.*

Finish in 4th position, with the arms lifted up (3rd position) – *in one beat.*

---

[5] The designation to this group of dance movements of the musical term "adagio" does not necessarily require the musical tempo "adagio"; other slow tempi may also be used, such as "andante", "moderato", etc.

V

Andante. M. ♩ = 42

ALLEGRO (JUMPS)

I.

4 measures of 2/4

1st measure – From 5th position in demi-plié, two ronds de jambe en l'air sauté with the right leg, done with a half-turn en dehors, and stop facing back – *on the 1st beat.*
Conclude with an assemblé, right foot front – *on the 2nd beat.*

2nd measure – The same again, with a half-turn en dehors, and finish facing the audience.

3rd measure – Double rond de jambe en l'air sauté en dehors twice, the first time executed from 5th position with a stop in 2nd position at 45° – *on the 1st beat.* The second time, repeat with temps levé – *on the 2nd beat.*

4th measure – Pas de bourrée en dehors, finishing in 5th position – *on the 3rd [1st] beat.*
Brisé front with the left leg to 5th position – *on the 4th [2nd] beat.*
The combination is done en dedans on the other leg, again i*n four measures.*

II.

4 measures of 2/4

1st measure – From 5th position in demi-plié, left foot front, rond de jambe en l'air sauté with a half-turn en dedans, stopping back – *on the 1st beat.*
Close with assemblé, left foot behind – *on the 2nd beat.*

2nd measure – Repeat with a half-turn, and finish facing the audience.

3rd measure – Double rond de jambe en l'air sauté en dedans – twice, the first done from 5th position and stopping in 2nd position at 45° – *on the 1st beat* – and repeat with temps levé – *on the 2nd beat.*

4th measure – Pas de bourrée en dedans, finishing in 5th position – *on the 3rd [1st] beat.*
Brisé back to 5th position with the right leg – *on the 4th [2nd] beat.*

I

II

III. CLASSROOM VARIATIONS

16 measures of 2/4

1st & 2nd measures	– 5th position demi-plié and, starting *on the up-beat*, glissade écarté front with the right leg, and do a grand jeté in 1st arabesque.
3rd & 4th measures	– Glissade in écarté back with the left leg, and grand jeté in effacé back (the right leg opening to effacé front).
5th & 6th measures	– Grande sissonne renversée en dehors, finishing in demi-plié on the right leg (the left foot sur le cou-de-pied).
7th & 8th measures	– Grand fouetté sauté en tournant en dedans with the left leg, finishing in 3rd arabesque.
9th & 10th measures	– Pas de bourrée en dedans and grand jeté in attitude effacée.
11th & 12th measures	– Repeat the previous movements.
13th, 14th, 15th & 16th measures	– Coupé on the left foot and tours chaînés on the diagonal toward point *2* (fig. 2b).

Repeat it all to the other side.

III

Allegro M.♩=120

Муз. П. Чаиковского *

* Music: P. Tchaikovsky

IV
Performed in a strict rhythmic pattern – 8 measures of 2/4

1st measure – 5th position, entrechat-cinq – left foot back (the right arm is in 1st position, the left in 2nd position) – *on the 1st beat.*

Pas de bourrée en dehors en tournant to 5th position – *on the 2nd beat;* in the turn, the arms close into preparatory position.

2nd measure – Entrechat-cinq, right foot back (the left arm is in 1st position, the right in 2nd) – *on the 1st beat.*

Pas de bourrée en dehors en tournant to 5th position – *on the 2nd beat;* in the turn, the arms close into preparatory position.

3rd measure – Entrechat-cinq, right foot front (the left arm is in 1st position, the right in 2nd position) – *on the 1st beat.*

Pas de bourrée en dedans en tournant to 5th position – *on the 2nd beat.*

(In the turn, the arms close into preparatory position.)

4th measure – Repeat the same with the other leg – *in two beats.*

5th measure – Two brisés front to the left leg – *in two beats* (the left arm is in 1st position, the right in 2nd position, without strain; in the first brisé, the palms face down, while in the second, they face up.)

6th measure – Two brisés back to the right leg – *in two beats* (the right arm is in 1st position, the left in 2nd position, with the hands as in the previous movement).

7th measure – Glissade with the left leg to 2nd position – *on the 1st beat.*

Entrechat-six de volée, left leg in écarté front (in the jump, the arms open to a pose écartée), and finish with the left foot front in 5th position – *on the 2nd beat.*

8th measure – Turn from 5th position, en dehors, changing feet (*both* arms are up) and finish in 5th position, right foot front, in demi-plié – *on the 2nd beat.*

IV

V
8 measures of 6/8

The direction is from point *6* to point *2* on the classroom diagram. Pose croisée back in demi-plié on the left leg (*before the first measure*).

1st measure – Jeté passé front with the right leg.

2nd measure – Repeat this step.

3rd measure – Sissonne tombée in effacé front to the right foot. Grand assemblé en tournant en dedans, finishing in 5th position, left foot front.

4th measure – Small sissonne tombée to the back in croisé with the left leg, and cabriole fermée at 45° with the right leg front toward point *8* (fig. 2b).

5th measure – Grand jeté in attitude croisée on the right leg, beginning it from a préparation coupé on the left leg.

6th measure – Repeat the same grand jeté.

7th measure – Sissonne tombée, left leg front in effacé, and grande cabriole in 1st arabesque on the left leg.

8th measure – Run, with the body facing the audience, to point *4*, and from there, begin the combination again with the other leg.

V

Allegro non tanto M.♩=60

Муз. П.Чайковского *

---

* Music: P. Tchaikovsky

REPEAT
ALL OF THE ABOVE
FROM POINT *4* TO POINT *8*
ON OUR CLASSROOM DIAGRAM

EXERCISES ON POINTE

I
8 measures of 2/4

1st measure – Two échappés in 2nd position with a change of feet – *in one beat each.*

2nd measure – Three sus-sous moving forward in croisé (right foot front) – *in three half-beats* – and *on the 4th half-beat*, stop in 5th position in demi-plié. (While executing this, the hands rise to a small pose, and the head is turned to the right.)

3rd measure – Two échappés in 2nd position with a change of feet – *in one beat each.*

4th measure – Three sus-sous moving to croisé back (left foot back), *in three half-beats*, stop in 5th position demi-plié *on the 4th half-beat* (with the head deflected slightly to the left and the gaze directed back over the left shoulder).

5th measure – Two sissonnes simples, to the right leg then the left, changing feet each time – *in one beat each.*

6th measure – Two ronds de jambe en l'air en dehors with the right leg, *on the 1st beat; on the 2nd beat*, [close into] 5th position in demi-plié, left leg front.

7th measure – Four sissonnes simples, changing feet each time, *in half-beats*, moving to the back, the last one ending in préparation in 4th position.

8th measure – Two tours en dehors sur le cou-de-pied *on the 1st beat*, finish *on the 2nd beat* in 4th position, with both arms up (and the gaze under the arm toward the left).

Repeat to the other side.

I

Allegro non troppo. M. ♩=52

II

8 measures of 3/8

1st measure – 1st position; right leg, three chassés forward in croisé on pointe *in three beats*, finishing in 5th position demi-plié. The right arm is lifted during the execution and gradually opens.

2nd measure – Left leg, assemblé soutenu en tournant (*in three beats*, the arms coming together in the turn).

3rd measure – Left leg, three chassés in croisé back on pointe *in three beats*, finishing in 5th position demi-plié; the left arm is lifted and opens gradually during the chassés.

4th measure – Right leg, assemblé soutenu en dehors en tournant *in three beats* (the arms come together in preparatory position).

5th, 6th, 7th measures – Temps couru on pointe en tournant en dedans, turning around [the body's] own axis, with the left leg front and the left arm lifted, *in two beats*; *on the 3rd beat*, place the right foot front in 5th position, the right arm in 1st position and the left in 2nd position. [Repeat on the 6th and 7th measures.]

8th measure[6] – Then a small pas de basque to préparation in 4th position, and two tours en dehors sur le cou-de-pied, all done *in three beats*.

III

8 measures of 6/8

1st, 2nd, 3rd & 4th measures – Do four grand fouettés en dehors in 2nd position at 90° – *in six beats each*, finishing in plié, with the right foot at the [left] knee.

5th measure – From here, take a half-turn en dedans on the right leg in 1st arabesque, and plié.
Another half-turn in 1st arabesque, finishing in plié.

6th measure – Two tours en dedans, with the left foot à la tire-bouchon, finishing on the left leg in demi-plié, the right foot sur le cou-de-pied.

7th measure – Step backward on pointe, *six times, one beat for each step*, changing feet [each time] (the arms are raised and gradually opened [lit.: revealed]).

8th measure – Préparation in 4th position, left foot front, and two tours en dehors sur le cou-de-pied. Finish in 4th position demi-plié, right foot back.

---

[6] This entire figure of movements should be performed without coming down [off pointe, facing] toward direction *2* of our classroom diagram.

* Music: Minkus

APPENDIX.
REFERENCES TO THE ITALIAN SCHOOL
by Alessandra Alberti

In her text, Agrippina Vaganova often makes specific references to the "Italian School", to "Italian technique", and indeed to Enrico Cecchetti himself, who, among his other activities, also taught at the Imperial School in St. Petersburg when Vaganova was still a student. To better illuminate some of these references to Cecchetti and some terminology from Cecchetti's method, we present here several of the passages to which Vaganova refers, together with explanatory notes, as well as brief terminological outlines from the official Cecchetti Method texts in use today.

For references to the Cecchetti Method texts, we have placed the respective page numbers in standard parentheses. The same is done for the relevant page numbers from Vaganova, with regard to those Cecchetti exercises or passages that find direct resonance in Vaganova's text.

Excerpts from the Cecchetti Method textbooks (see list below) are enclosed in quotation marks for clarity*. Supplementary comments in italics are those of the author (A. A.).

The illustrations are those by Randolph Schwabe that originally accompanied the first edition of Beaumont and Idzikowski's *Manual* of 1922, which Vaganova knew well enough to even include in her text (fig. 55, p. 126). The numbering of these illustrations has been adjusted here, as have references to these pages in the quoted text.

Please note that the system used here to enumerate the points of the room is that of the Cecchetti tradition (see p. 246).

BEAUMONT, CYRIL W. and IDZIKOWSKI, STANISLAS, *A Manual of the Theory and Practice of Classical Theatrical Dancing (Cecchetti Method)*, C. W. Beaumont, London, 1922, and I.S.T.D., London, 1977.

CRASKE, MARGARET and BEAUMONT, CYRIL W., *The Theory and Practice of Allegro in Classical Ballet (Cecchetti Method)*, C. W. Beaumont, London, 1930, reprinted 1972.

CRASKE, MARGARET and De Moroda, Derra, *The Theory and Practice of Advanced Allegro in Classical Ballet (Cecchetti Method)*, I.S.T.D., London, 1956 and 1979.

---

* The Cecchetti texts are reprinted here in the form in which they appear in the respective manuals, with the original punctuation and use of bold and italics. *Ed.*

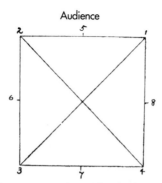

The directions according to the Cecchetti Method

Second *pointe tendue*   Second *en l'air*   Second *en l'air,*
                                                          demi-position

Positions of the Legs (relative to height)

(from Beaumont's *Manual*, pp. 21, 22)
"...**à terre** (that is, on the ground), **pointe tendue** (that is, with the toe stretched), **en l'air** (that is, in the air), and **en l'air, demi-position** (that is, in the air, half-way position).
When the entire base of the foot touches the ground, the foot is said to be *à terre*...
If, however, we say open the *right* foot to the *second* position, **pointe tendue**, the pupil will... [be] forcing the instep well outwards, so that the sole is raised to such a degree that only the tips of the toes rest on the floor...
Again, if the foot is... raised until [it] is at right angles to the hip, the foot is said to be in the *second* position, **en l'air**...

Finally, if the foot… is then slowly raised until [it] is **halfway** between the *second* position*, pointe tendue*, and the *second* position, *en l'air*, the foot is said to be in the *second* position, *en l'air* (**demi-position**)."

Positions of the Arms
(from Beaumont's *Manual*, pp. 24, 25)

"There are **five** principal positions of the arms:-
(i) **1st Position**. – See Fig. 19.
(ii) **2nd Position**. – See Fig. 20.
(iii) **3rd Position**. – See Fig. 21…
(iv) **4th Position**. – See Fig. 22a…
(v) **5th Position**. – See Fig. 23a.

Note that in the **first** position, the hands are held at the sides with the finger-tips near the outside of the thigh… [*Editor's note: The 1922 edition quaintly describes this position as being "…with the fingertips just touching the seam of the knickers".*]

Whenever an arm is rounded in front of the body, as in the *third, fourth,* or *fifth* positions, it should be extended as much as possible (always preserving a rounded appearance), be in a line with the fork of the ribs, and it must **not pass beyond an imaginary line drawn down the centre of the body.** Again, when one or both arms are rounded above the head, the arm or arms should be rounded so that the point of the elbow is imperceptible; and if the eyes are raised, the finger-tips of the hand or hands should be just within the range of vision. Finally, when both arms are rounded above the head or in front of the body, the finger-tips should be separated by a distance of four inches…

…In order to distinguish the *fourth* position shown in Fig. 22a from that shown in Fig. 22b, these positions are qualified respectively with the terms *en haut*, that is, *high*; and *en avant*, that is, *forwards*…

The three variants of the *fifth* position as shown in Figs. 23a, 23b and 23c are distinguished respectively by the terms *en avant, en haut,* and *en bas*, that is, *low*.

Fig. 24b shows… *demi-seconde* position… It will be noticed that it is situated between the *first* and *second* positions…"

The Positions of the Arms
in the Cecchetti Method

Fig. 19. First

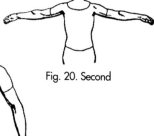

Fig. 20. Second

Fig. 21. Third

Fig. 22a. Fourth *en haut*

Fig. 22b. Fourth *en avant*

Fig. 23a. Fifth *en avant*

Fig. 23b. Fifth *en haut*

Fig. 23c. Fifth *en bas*

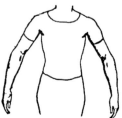

Fig. 24b. Demi-seconde

Attitude Croisée and Arabesques
in the Cecchetti Method

Fig. 35. Attitude croisée

Fig. 36. First

Fig. 37. Second

Fig. 38. Third

Fig. 39. Fourth

Fig. 40. Fifth

The Directions of the Body
in the Cecchetti Method

Fig. 42. *À la quatrième devant*

Fig. 41. *Croisé devant*

Fig. 43. *Écarté*

Fig. 44. *Effacé*

Fig. 45. *À la seconde*

Fig. 46. *Épaulé*

Fig. 47. *À la quatrième derrière*

Fig. 48.
Croisé derrière

Arabesques
(from Beaumont's *Manual*, p. 31)

"There are **five** principal arabesques.
(i) **First Arabesque** (see Fig. 36).
(ii) **Second Arabesque** (see Fig. 37).
(iii) **Third Arabesque** (see Fig. 38).
(iv) **Fourth Arabesque** (see Fig. 39).
(v) **Fifth Arabesque** (see Fig. 40).
Note that the shoulders are held square to the line of direction, and that the hand extended in the *fourth* position *front* must always be in line with the shoulder at eye level. The arm extended in the *fourth* position *back* is disposed in the same line…"

Cecchetti's 2nd Port de Bras
(Vaganova's 4th port de bras, pp. 91-93 and Fig. 30)

(from Beaumont's *Manual*, pp. 84-85)
"The direction of the body is *croisé*.
1. Raise the arms to the *fifth* position *en avant* so that they face 2.
2. Raise the *left* arm above the head so that it faces 2.
   [*The entire arm is rotated so that the fingers are pointing up, the elbow points downward, and the palm faces toward the dancer.*]
   Move the *right* arm between the *demi-seconde* position and the *fourth* position *back*, so that it points to 4.
   (The arms are *en attitude*.) [*as in Fig. 35*]
   Bring the head upright and look towards the *left* hand.
3. Move the *left* arm downwards and backwards, passing through the *second* position, so that it is extended in the *fourth* position *back*, pointing to 4.
   Move the *right* arm forwards and upwards[1], passing through the *second* position, so that it is extended in the *fourth* position *front*, pointing to 2.
   Incline the head towards 1.
   (The arms are *en deuxième arabesque*.)

   [1] The arms must be moved in such a manner that as the *left* arm is lowered, the *right* arm is raised in proportion; the arms arrive simultaneously in the *second* position.

4. Lower the *left* arm to the first position, pass it to the *fifth* position *en bas*, and then raise it to the *fourth* position *en avant*.

Curve the *right* arm inwards and downwards so that the arms meet in the *fifth* position *en avant*.
5. Repeat 2."

Cecchetti's Grande Préparation pour Pirouettes en Dedans
(Vaganova's 6th port de bras, p. 94 and Fig. 32)

Although Vaganova does not expressly refer to Cecchetti's "Grande préparation pour pirouettes en dedans" in her text, it is interesting to note the elements in it that resonate in Vaganova's 6th port de bras.

[Prepare in croisé facing 1 (see diagram), right foot pointe tendue to the back, arms in attitude croisée, with the right arm high. Plié on the supporting leg, raise the back leg in attitude croisée, and at the same time:]

(from Craske and De Moroda, p. 83)
"(a) *Relevé* on *left* foot *sur la demi-pointe*.
(b) Lower *left* heel to the ground, allowing the knee to bend.
Extend *right* leg *en arabesque*.
Lower the *right* arm to *fourth* position *en avant*.
Carry the *left* arm through *first* position to *fourth* position *en avant*.
The arms must reach the *fifth* position *en avant* at the same time as the *demi-plié* on the *left* foot.
(c) Lower the *right* foot to *fourth* position *back*.
Straighten the *left* knee.
Raise the *left* arm to *fourth* position *en haut*, back of hand facing 1.
Sweep the *right* arm backwards towards 3, *en arabesque*.
Incline the head towards *left* shoulder.
(d) Lower *left* arm to *second* position, raise *right* arm to *second* position.
Lower *left* arm to *first* position – *fifth* position *en bas* and raise it to *fourth* position *en avant*.
Demi-plié on both feet."

Vaganova's 6th port de bras displays an affinity to the concept of the transfer of weight that is also evident in Cecchetti's "Grande préparation pour pirouettes en dedans", although Vaganova eliminates the attitude relevée croisé: the foot brushes the floor directly, forming a diagonal that begins at the head and continues all the way to the pointed toes of the back foot, which touches the floor. In the Cecchetti version, the body's diagonal is instead formed in the air, in an arabesque in plié, with the working leg en l'air. In Vaganova's 6th port de bras, there is effectively a change of weight from one leg to the other, while in her alternative version – the preparatory port de bras for big turns – the weight is transferred from one leg to two, in order to carry out the big fourth position preparation for turns. In Cecchetti's "Grande préparation pour pirouettes en dedans", the weight is also changed from one leg to two, using however a regular fourth position with both knees stretched.

Italian Jumps

(Vaganova's Grand changement de pieds and pas assemblé, pp. 122 and 125 and Fig's 51a, 55)

The following description applies to Cecchetti's grand assemblé dessus, but also to his grand jeté à la seconde, ballotté en avant and grand changement, in which the legs behave in the same way, with the toes of both feet drawn together while the body is still in the air.

(from Craske and Beaumont, p. 15)

"…

Exactly as the *right* foot rises to the *second* position, *en l'air*–
Leap upwards into the air off the *left* foot.
While the body is in the air–

(*b*) Bend both knees (a *plié a quart*) and bring together the flat of the toes of both feet.

(*c*) Come to the ground–allowing the knees to bend–with the feet in the *fifth* position, *right* foot *front*, and lower the heels to the ground…"

Landing from Jumps

(Vaganova's Grand changement de pieds, pp. 122 [see also note], 126, and Fig's 51a and 55)

In executing Cecchetti's grand assemblé, after having bent both knees (plié à quart) and drawn together "the flat of the toes of both feet" in the air, at the moment of landing, the feet pass first sur les demi-pointes, and then the heels are immediately placed on the floor, as can be seen in illustration Fig. 55 of Vaganova, which was extracted from Beaumont and Idzikowski's Manual.

(from Craske and Beaumont, p. 9)
"In alighting after a *pas d'élévation*, the tips of the toes should be the first to reach the ground, the sole of the foot following immediately, taking care that the heel is always *completely* lowered. Failure to lower the heel and to take a strong *demi-plié* results in a loss of *ballon*, that is, the smooth falling and rising of the feet in the passage from step to step."

Rising to Pointe

(Vaganova's Pointe-work, p. 171)

(from Craske and Beaumont, p. 30)
"Echappé sur les pointes.
... 1. *Demi-pliez* on both feet and, with a little spring, *instantaneously*–
   Open the feet *sur les pointes* in the *second* position...
  2. With a little spring, return to the *fifth* position..."

(from Craske and Beaumont, p. 86)
Relevé devant
[*from a demi-plié on both feet*]
"With a little spring, rise onto the *left pointe*, sharply straightening the knee.
Bring the *right pointe* in front of and in a line with the centre of the *left* knee..."

Turning Technique

(Vaganova's Tours from 4th position, p. 184)

(from Beaumont's *Manual*, p. 199)
"You have seen that the body is supported entirely on the *demi-pointe* of one foot. Consider how slight is the base upon which the whole body turns. For this reason you must press strongly against the ground all the toes of the supporting foot, so that by their expansion you will increase the size of the base and thereby materially assist the equilibrium of the body."

(from Craske and De Moroda, p. 82)
"All Centre *Pirouettes* should be learned on *pied à quart*.
   In some instances, when the foot is sufficiently strong they can be performed by women *sur la pointe*...
   ... It is usual to take the foot *sur le cou-de-pied* if one turn is done, and to the front of the supporting knee if more turns are done."

The Arms in Pirouettes

(Vaganova's Tours from 5th position, p. 186)

(from Beaumont's *Manual*, p. 199)

"...great care should be exercised in the force of momentum generated by the sweep across of the extended arm. Insufficient strength will cause the body to stop before the completion of the turn, conversely, too much strength will cause the body to pass beyond the point desired. The position of the arms in a **pirouette** is between the fifth position **en bas** and the fifth position **en avant**, although it is usually described as the fifth position **en bas**."

Cecchetti's Grande Préparation pour Pirouettes en Dehors

(Vaganova's Tours à la seconde at 90°, p. 189)

(from Craske and De Moroda, p. 82)

"Stand in the centre of the room, face 5. Feet in *fifth* position, *right* foot *front.*

Arms in *fifth* position *en bas.*

(*a*) Rise *sur les demi-pointes.*
   Raise the arms to *fifth* position *en avant.*

(*b*) Lower both heels. Keep arms in *fifth* position *en avant.*

(*c*) *Demi-plié* and open the right foot to *second* position, slightly off the floor (as in *battement dégagé*).

(*&*) *Relevé* on *left demi-pointe.*

(*d*) Lower the *left* heel. Lower the *right* foot to *second* position and immediately *demi-plié* with both feet.
   Carry the *right* arm to *fourth* position *en avant.*"

Italian Fouetté

(Vaganova's Grand Fouetté, pp. 200-01)

The "Italian fouetté" referred to by Vaganova appears in Cecchetti in a jumped version. The following description is extracted from the exercise "Fouetté sauté à six temps n° 2 en avant", of which the movement is part.

(from Craske and De Moroda, p. 72)

"Stand in the centre of the room, face 5. Feet in *fourth* position, *right* foot *back, pointe tendue*. Arms in *fifth* position *en bas*.

1. TEMPS LEVÉ WITH DÉVELOPPÉ – TEMPS LEVÉ WITH GRAND ROND DE JAMBE EN DEHORS

(a) *Temps levé* on *left* foot.
Développé with *right* leg to *quatrième position devant en l'air*.
Raise the arms to *fifth* position.
Opening *right* arm to *second* position.

(b) *Temps levé* on *left* foot.
Grand rond de jambe en dehors with *right* leg.
Raise the *left* arm to *fourth* position *en haut*.
Lower the *left* arm to *second* position.
Raise the *right* arm to *fourth* position *en haut*.

(c) Come to the ground on *left* foot, allowing the knee to bend.
Leave *right* leg *en arabesque*.
Lower the *right* arm to *fourth* position *en avant* and extend it to 5.
Carry the *left* arm backwards *en arabesque* to 7.
The position is *en arabesque*.
Note: The arm movements must be done in one sweeping movement."

Grand Fouetté

(Vaganova's Grand Fouetté, pp. 200-01)

The Cecchetti equivalent of Vaganova's grand fouetté can be found in the Manual as part of the adagio called "FOUETTÉ ET BALLOTTÉ".

(from Beaumont's *Manual*, pp. 176-77)
"…

5. **Développé à la quatrième devant en l'air (effacée)**
with the *right* foot.

(a) As the *right* foot rises in line with the *left* knee –
Raise the arms to the *fifth* position *en avant*.

(b) As the foot is extended to the *fourth* position *front, en l'air*, pointing to 1 –
Open the *right* arm to the *second* position.
Incline the head to 2 [*simultaneously*].

6. *Demi-pliez* on the *left* foot.
7. In one sweeping movement –
   Turn slightly to the left, so that the body faces 5.
   Straighten the *left* knee and rise *sur la demi-pointe*.
   Move the *right* foot to the *second* position, *en l'air.*
   Raise the *left* arm in semi-circular movement so that it passes
   above the head and then to the *second* position.
   Raise the *right* arm to the *fourth* position *en haut.*
   Bring the head erect.
   Lower the left heel to the ground.
8. Turn to the *left* on the flat of the *left* foot, so that the body
   faces 2.
   Pass the *right* foot *à l'attitude.*
   Lower the *left* arm to *demi-seconde* position.
   The pose is *en attitude.*"

ANALYTICAL INDEXES

Names and Titles from Introductory Forwards and Appendix

**Technical Terminology, Names and Titles
from Vaganova's Prefaces and Main Text**

FLAVIA PAPPACENA was Professor of Dance Theory and Dance Aesthetics at the National Academy of Dance in Rome from 1974-2012 and at the Literature Faculty of the University of Rome *La Sapienza* from 2006-2014. She has directed the dance section at Gremese publishers since 1984 and is the founding director of the research journal *Chorégraphie*. Author of numerous technical manuals on dance for Gremese, she has also penned many essays and books of historical and theoretic nature, including: *Excelsior: Documents and Essays; Carlo Blasis' Treatise on Dance 1820-1830;* and *The Language of Classical Ballet.* She has edited critical editions of *La Sténochorégraphie* by Arthur Saint-Léon, Jean-Georges Noverre's *Lettres sur la danse et sur les ballets (1803)* and the two volumes of Grazioso Cecchetti's book *Classical Dance. A Complete Manual of the Cecchetti Method.*

BRUCE MICHELSON studied at the Pennsylvania Ballet School and performed worldwide as a dancer with major American and European dance companies, including Pittsburgh Ballet Theatre, Hamburg Ballet, Ballet Rambert, Geneva Ballet and Nederlands Dans Theater. He was Balletmaster with both the Zurich Ballet and Ballet Gulbenkian, and has been an international guest teacher and choreographic assistant since 2000. Correspondent for *Dance Europe* magazine since 2003, he also writes for the Czech magazine *Taneční Zóna* and has translated numerous dance texts from various languages into English, including articles for the German magazine *ballett-tanz* and Flavia Pappacena's *The Language of Classical Ballet* (2012).

ALESSANDRA ALBERTI graduated from the National Academy of Dance in Rome, where she also taught ballet technique from 1990 to 1995. She attended Maurice Béjart's Mudra school and danced professionally with the Hamburg Ballet, the Teatro Comunale in Bologna, Balletto di Spoleto and the Zurich Ballet. She is an I.S.T.D. Licentiate and Tutor in the Cecchetti Method and has collaborated with Flavia Pappacena on various technical manuals and historical dance publications. Guest teacher in Switzerland, Portugal, Germany, The Netherlands and the U.S., she has co-directed The Hamlyn School in Florence since 2000.

ALEKSANDR WILANSKY was trained in the Vaganova and Tarasov Methods. He studied the Diaghilev-era repertoire while in London and became an acknowledged expert in this field. He was assistant to Nicolai Beriosoff, and, as an officer in U.N.E.S.C.O.'s *Comité Nijinsky*, organized exhibitions and performances for the Nijinsky Centenary Celebrations. He has written for magazines such as *Dance and Dancers* and co-authored books including *Ecrits sur Nijinsky* and *Nijinsky, un dieu danse à travers moi.* In 1996, the Polish Government honored him with the Nijinsky Medal, in recognition of his life's work in preserving, producing and educating in the world of dance.